Situating Readers

Situating Readers

Students Making Meaning of Literature

Harold A. Vine, Jr.
New York University

Mark A. Faust
University of Georgia

National Council of Teachers of English
1111 W. Kenyon Road, Urbana, Illinois 61801-1096

To Dora and Harold Vine, and Carolyn and Amy—HAV

To Jody and Richard Faust, and Elise and Victoria—MAF

Grateful acknowledgment is made for permission to reprint "Reel One" by Adrien Stoutenburg, from *Heroes, Advise Us,* published by Charles Scribner's Sons, 1964. Copyright © 1964 by Adrien Stoutenburg. Reprinted with permission of Curtis Brown, Ltd.

NCTE Editorial Board: Keith Gilyard, Ronald Jobe, Joyce Kinkead, Louise Phelps, Gladys Veidemanis, Charles Suhor, *chair, ex officio,* and Michael Spooner, *ex officio*

Manuscript Editor: Jane M. Curran

Staff Editor: Marlo Welshons

Cover Design: Doug Burnett

Interior Book Design: Doug Burnett

NCTE Stock Number: 44764-3050

Library of Congress Cataloging-in-Publication Data

Vine, Harold A., 1933–
    Situating readers : students making meaning of literature / Harold A. Vine, Jr., Mark A. Faust.
       p.   cm.
    Includes bibliographical references.
    ISBN 0-8141-4476-4
    1. Literature—Study and teaching. 2. Reading. I. Faust, Mark A., 1957– .
    II. Title.
PN61.V56   1993
807—dc20
                                        93-7889
                                            CIP

Contents

Acknowledgments

Without the thoughtful cooperation of the 288 students who shared with us their readings of "Reel One," *Situating Readers* would have remained no more than an intriguing prospect. Our thanks to each of these students and to our colleagues Elizabeth Lawrence, Roz Mazzalupo, and Mary Rooney, who helped us gather many of these readings. Our appreciation as well to Adrien Stoutenburg for writing such a continually fascinating poem.

To thank all who in any way contributed to our research would be impossible here, but we would like to mention the names of those who contributed directly to the ideas, content, and organization of the book. Our thanks to Gordon Pradl, professor of English Education at New York University, for his wonderful suggestions on how to select the student readings to be discussed and how to present our interpretations of those readings; Andrew Gottlieb, colleague and friend, whose theory of "imagining upon the imagined" contributed so much to our thinking; and John Anzul, Joni Babalis, Isis Costa, Mindy Meyers, Candice Oen, Rebecca Packer, Sarah Pierson, Elizabeth Prohaska, and the students enrolled in "Reading and Literature with Adolescents" (fall 1990) for reading various versions of this book and making such valuable suggestions.

We feel most fortunate to have had the wonderful editorial assistance of Michael Spooner and Jane Curran of NCTE.

We appreciate the encouragement and support of our university colleagues: Nancy Lester, John Mayher, Marilyn Sobelman (New York University), Hugh Agee, Lee Galda, Ron Kieffer, Sally Ross, Joel Taxel (University of Georgia), and Anna Soter (Ohio State University), for their willingness to discuss many of the ideas we present in this book and their continuing and invaluable support; and Ann Marcus, Gabe Carras, Mark Alter, Elmer Baker, and Roger Cayer—NYU administrators present and past—who, in numerous ways, enabled our research efforts.

We are grateful to Valerie Walsh for allowing us to publish parts of her own research on the potential role of writing in assessing learnings from literature.

We wish to express our appreciation to Margaret Early and Ben Nelms (University of Florida) for their enthusiastic response to our book and for their efforts in disseminating salient aspects of our research to readers of *English Journal*. Excerpts from the book appeared in the November 1992 (vol. 81, no. 7) through April 1993 (vol. 82, no. 4) issues of *English Journal*.

We are thankful for all of our students over the years, whose readings, writings, and conversations have continually enabled us to develop as teachers and persons.

Finally, we are deeply grateful for our immediate and extended circle of family and friends without whose love and concern throughout the years we would have accomplished nothing.

I Introduction

1 Beginning Reflections and Invitation

For forty-four combined years of teaching—in high schools, colleges, and universities—we have been trying to empower students as readers of literature. Initially, we were not very successful. But by continually revising our practice and striving to understand students' readings, we have, over time, developed an approach for empowering readers. Although we still have questions about our theory and practice, we believe that we have made enough significant discoveries to warrant sharing them with others. We have written this short book, therefore, to invite you to participate in a portion of our journey, to explore some of our findings, and to join with us in our ongoing efforts to empower all persons as meaning makers.

Since our stance has changed dramatically over time, let us share a glimpse of the distance that we have traveled in order to arrive at our present concerns. When we began teaching, we believed that we were empowering our students by giving to them—in the manner of most of our college teachers—a critically approved interpretation of each work. Sometimes we were so unsure of our own interpretations and so concerned that students get what we considered to be the most acceptable interpretations that we did not even bother with how we made sense of the text, seeking instead only the written opinions of critics. Then by lecturing or conducting closely guided recitations, we ensured that all students received the accepted interpretation. As for students' readings, we were as unaware of them as we were of our own.

But we did not remain unaware for long. When some students asked us how we had arrived at a proffered interpretation, when other students offered alternative interpretations, and when we then began to reflect on how much we had disliked being given interpretations by our English professors, we decided to modify our practice. At the same time we were reading and being impressed by those reader-oriented theorists, especially Louise Rosenblatt, who insisted that the *lived-through experience* of reading literature was more important than the production of authoritative theme statements. These writings prompted us to ask: What constitutes the moment-by-moment evocation of a reading event, and what bearing, if any, does this have on our theory and practice of teaching reading and literature? How might we reconcile this concern for the reader's *lived-through experience* with our sense of responsibility to authors and their texts? And if we have a *responsibility* as readers, how might this responsibility be defined without limiting our role to that of being passive consumers of someone else's interpretations? We then began to pay attention to our own lived-through experiences of the works we were teaching.

Harold's approach to Thornton Wilder's *Our Town* with a group of sixteen year olds typifies this second stage of our teaching. The students were expected to read the play on their own and then participate in a sequence of activities carefully orchestrated to produce a predetermined outcome: experiencing *Our Town* as embodying the theme *living life in the context of eternity.* This sequence of events was so successful in bringing about the desired reader response that— years later—some students still recall and talk about the experience. And why had Harold interpreted the work as embodying the theme *living life in the context of eternity*? Because that was the concern he had experienced with that play at that time.

We did not routinely engineer such successes with the works that we were teaching, but the *Our Town* experience illustrates the ideal that we sought at that time. We assumed that it was our responsibility to make literature meaningful for our students, and we wanted to make sure that students experienced the work in the same way that we had. But we did not realize that we were also assuming that our students were incapable of generating powerful experiences on their own. Had we thought about this, we might have realized that in making our interpretations and the teaching of them the center of attention, we were doing little to understand and empower our students as readers.

We cannot trace with certainty all the variables that prompted our next period of development, but we can mention several key factors. Students' responses to our occasional open-ended reading assignments, for instance, often revealed insights that we had not sensed in our interpretation of the work. Also, we discovered casebooks containing dozens of different interpretations of the same text, and we used these to broaden both our own and our students' understand- ings of a work. Furthermore, we read about and began to use all sorts of ways for helping students express their responses to a text. As a result, over time, we became more and more dissatisfied with the quizzes, thesis papers, and final exams that we had been using. Our earlier desire to wrap up a work and grade all readings according to the same standard gave way to our developing sense of the multiplicity of meaningful readings and the impossibility of bringing interpretation to a close.

During this third phase of our teaching, we used a variety of reader-based approaches. First, we sought to begin with students' initial responses to the text: responses that were written and kept by the student, written and given to us, written and shared orally with the entire class, or written and shared in small groups, or just presented orally. This was easy to do, and students enjoyed sharing their initial meaning makings with each other. But these ways of sharing did not produce what we considered to be sufficient learning.

Second, we tried using readers' initial interpretations as the basis for making decisions about where we would go next in our meaning making. In one of our earliest attempts, we allowed students to have a free-flowing discussion based on their initial responses to the text. In another early approach, we had students begin to share their initial responses with the whole class; then we latched onto one or two that we considered problematic, and we led students to see how the text could be better interpreted. Realizing that this was not greatly different from our earlier ways of teaching—except that we were basing our teaching on a brief diagnosis of students' *problems*—we gradually abandoned these approaches. Sometimes we allowed students to meet in small groups to share and discuss their initial responses to the text, in the belief that fewer students talking together would produce more meaning making. Sometimes the results of these small-group discussions were rewarding; sometimes they were not. Eventually, we concluded, just having students meet in small groups to discuss a text is not enough. Most often we tried to analyze students' initial interpretations and decide where to go from there. But when students shared their initial responses with the entire class, we usually found ourselves unable to sort through the cacophony of differing perspectives. Finally, we experimented with guiding students to formulate their questions about the work. And when we realized that students did not know how to ask questions that were both sufficiently focused and open-ended, we proceeded to teach them how to create such questions for enabling effective meaning making. This seemed to be the solution to our problem—except for the fact that students often asked teacher-type questions in which they had little interest.

The third approach that we attempted in our reader-based curriculum was to have students do creative projects as a way of summarizing a unit of work—instead of taking tests or writing literary criticism papers. Students enjoyed doing these projects: making collages, creating and performing scripts based on or related to the texts, transforming the work into a different genre, putting the characters on trial, writing letters to the author. But more often than not, we were unable to ascertain as fully as we wished just what students were learning as a result of their efforts.

As we write about our problems in trying to create a reader-based curriculum, we can appreciate why so many teachers do not even try to do this, and why so many other teachers decry such an approach. After all, when teachers begin with a text and a critic's or their own interpretation of this text, it is relatively easy to design lessons to lead students to predetermined conclusions. But when teachers try to begin with and build from students' initial interpretations of a text, the task is infinitely harder. For some teachers, a reader-based classroom is difficult because they cannot tolerate not knowing exactly where they are going and what students will be learning. Other teachers cannot tolerate such a classroom because it violates their sense of themselves as the seat of knowledge and power, and they do not believe students can learn anything of much value by themselves. Neither of these issues was a problem for us. We enjoyed going into the classroom and allowing the curriculum to unfold organically from our students, and we believed that students ultimately could take responsibility for their own learning—if given the necessary support and guidance. But we remained unsure about how to provide that support and guidance. What we found so difficult about teaching in a reader-based classroom was our inability to understand, as fully as we wanted to, how our students were going about making sense of texts, and how such reading abilities grew and developed over time.

In an effort to gain a better understanding of our students' ways of reading, we turned to what others had said about students' responses to texts. This professional literature confirmed what we had already discovered about the role of the reader: that the reader's gender, ethnicity, beliefs, linguistic abilities, values, concerns, and backgrounds of experience affect how he or she reads a text.[1] It also gave us a few ways of identifying readers' problems and categorizing readers' responses.[2] But none of these findings helped us make adequate sense of our students' interpretations. Also, we read widely the works of literary theorists who sought to describe the ways in which ideal and theoretical readers read, usually citing their own professional readings as examples. We found it useful to hear that authors leave gaps that readers are invited to fill (Iser 1976); that the meaning of a work of literature is not some theme statement to be extracted upon finishing a text but the experience of having lived through the work (Rosenblatt [1938] 1976, 1978; Fish 1980, 21–67); and that reading is more a political act than one of ascertaining an author's true meaning (Eagleton 1983; Mailloux 1989). Despite our extensive research, we still had an incomplete understanding of how *our students*—nonprofessional readers—were making sense of the texts that they were reading. At this point in our teaching, we decided to conduct our own research, seeking answers to the following questions:

- How do students go about making sense of a text?
- What disempowers meaning making?
- What empowers meaning making?
- How might we empower readers in our classroom?

In part two of this book, we inductively explore possible answers to our first question. In part three, we share with you what our research suggests are possible answers to the remaining three questions.

Because we wanted to understand not only an individual student's meaning making but also how readers develop over time, we chose a method for investigating how readers ranging from junior high school to graduate school read the same text. To accomplish this, we needed a text easy enough for our youngest readers, yet challenging enough for our oldest. For this reason, we selected a text that we knew from experience would be engaging for a variety of readers: Adrien Stoutenburg's "Reel One."

Having determined our research goals and selected a text that our range of readers could read, we had to decide how to collect the student readings. Should readers read the text for themselves? Orally or silently? Once or more than once? Should readers be allowed to respond freely, be asked specific questions, or both? Should readers' responses be oral, written, or both? If readers are to respond orally, should they be given instruction and practice, be told how and when to respond, be accompanied by an adult? If readers are to respond in writing, what questions should they be asked, what form should the writing take, what might be done to enable fluency and alleviate anxiety? Should the data collection occur at home or in school, be timed or untimed?

Because we wanted approximately fifty readings from students at each of four different age levels (11–12, 14–15, 17–18, and 20–25), we chose to have the data collected in school, during the students' regular English class, by the students' regular English teacher, giving students written directions to read the text silently and to write answers to a couple of open-ended questions. To engage students in our research, we presented it as an experiment called "Exploration: A Slow-Motion Study of How I Re-create a Poem." (In light of our research, we wish that we had used the term *co-create*, instead of *re-create*.) To encourage students to write specifically about both the text and themselves, we asked students to "write down your observations and thoughts about the poem." To investigate how individual readings develop over time, we asked students to read and write about the text three times. And because we believe that most of our thinking about texts (stories, television shows, movies, people) occurs without the actual physical text being present, we asked students to do each writing about the text from memory. In addition, wanting to see what readers think about their reading processes, we asked them to "write about how you went about re-creating 'Reel One.'" Throughout the experiment, students were allowed enough time so that the vast majority were able to write all they wanted in answer to our questions. After collecting what our students had written about "Reel One," typing the writings so that they could be more easily read, correcting obvious misspellings and omissions of punctuation so that we could concentrate on content, and changing students' names to ensure anonymity, we tried to make sense of what these nonprofessional readers were doing.

Had we known then how challenging it would be to make sense of our readers' readings, this book might never have been written. Indeed, we spent years sifting and sorting through the hundreds of readings that we had collected, wearing out one interpretative scheme[3] after another as we sought to bring into focus what seemed to us a bewildering multiplicity of experiences with "Reel One." Ultimately, by revising our questions and ways of conceptualizing reading (Faust 1990), we arrived at our present hypothesis: *reading is sensing and making sense of situations.*[4] Once we began to regard reading as sensing and making sense of a situation, the similarities and differences among our many protocols began to appear less bewildering.

Then we had to select which of the 288 sets of readings we were going to analyze for this book. Heeding the advice of a colleague, we selected groups of responses that engaged us, agreed to explore these readings through oral dialogue, and recorded our in-depth conversations about how we sensed that these readers were making meaning through sensing and making sense of a situation. Overall, we tried to find a way of talking about these readings that would validate the accomplishments of these readers and, at the same time, offer paths toward improvement. Our conversations proved so successful that we have included six of them—in revised form—in part two of this book. We present our efforts in dialogue form in order to demonstrate the developmental nature of our explorations, to make it easier for you to situate yourself in relation to our own and our students' voices, and to illustrate the values of collaborative meaning making.

Throughout our book, we endeavor to situate our readers by understanding as empathetically as possible what each was doing, how, and why. At the same time, we are suggesting that truly empowered readers are able to situate themselves during the act of reading. Finally, we believe that teachers are responsible for situating readers in such a way that students' natural capacities to sense and make sense of situations are supported and extended.

If there is an element of persuasion in the way that we have edited our conversations, it derives from our conviction that most of these students did generate meaningful readings, and from our hypotheses about what empowered them. At the same time, you will notice our discomfort as we point out reading strategies and assumptions that seem to be inhibiting and even disempowering for some readers. As we explore these students' beginning moves toward meaning making, we believe that what initially empowers the interpretations of nonprofessional readers is essentially similar to what empowers the interpretations of professionals. Of course, you, our readers, are free to decide whether you think our interpretations are persuasive.

Reading can be, simultaneously, both an intensely private and an engagingly social experience. We believe that this accounts in part for why we are drawn to the experience that reading offers. Through reading and sharing our readings we can become more understanding of others as we become more understanding of ourselves. In the past, we felt burdened by customary ways of defining what the *it* is that we should talk about when we talked about literature. Too often, we sensed that something was lost as we sought to negotiate conflicting demands. On the one hand, we wanted to encourage *responsive* reading; on the other, we wanted to ensure *responsible* reading. We hope that *Situating Readers* helps you, as it has helped us, to see that it is possible to avoid this painful dilemma if we more fully situate ourselves and our students in a collaborative endeavor to enjoy reading, to better understand others and ourselves, and to be empowered readers.

Now we invite you to join in our exploration. To enable you to do this and to be respectful of our student readers, the sets of student readings reported in part two of this book are presented in full, and without interruption or an intitial interpretation from us. In this way, we encouage you to make sense of these readings for yourself, before noting what we have to say. Also, we hope that you will join in our developing dialogue, both individually and with your colleagues. Finally, we ask you to begin—as we, ourselves, did—by reading and writing about "Reel One." Start by reading the poem presented in figure 1. Then follow the directions given in figure 2. In this way you will be better prepared to make sense of what the readers in our study were asked to do, and what they accomplished.

Reel One

It was all technicolor
from bullets to nurses.
The guns gleamed like cars
and blood was as red
as the paint on dancers.
The screen shook with fire
and my bones whistled.
It was like life, but better.

I held my girl's hand,
in the deepest parts,
and we walked home, after,
with the snow falling,
but there wasn't much blue
in the drifts or corners:
just white and more white
and the sound track so dead
you could almost imagine
the trees were talking.

—Adrien Stoutenburg

Reprinted by permission of Curtis Brown, Ltd. From *Heroes, Advise Us*, published by Charles Scribner's Sons, 1964. Copyright © 1964 by Adrien Stoutenburg.

Figure 1. Copy of "Reel One" by Adrien Stoutenburg that was given to students to read.

Exploration: A Slow-Motion Study of How I Re-create a Poem

This exploration is designed to help you see how you go about re-creating a work of literature.

1a. Thoroughly read Adrien Stoutenburg's "Reel One."

1b. Then turn the poem face down, and write down your observations and thoughts about the poem.

2a. Read "Reel One" for a second time.

2b. Then turn the poem face down, and again write down all your observations and thoughts about the poem. When you've run out of everything to say—

3a. Read "Reel One" for a third time.

3b. Then turn the poem face down, and again write down all your final observations and thoughts about the poem.

Note: Make sure to number your sheets of paper and to indicate which is your 1st, 2d, and 3d set of writings about the poem.

4. Finally, re-read what you have written. Then write about how you went about re-creating "Reel One."

Figure 2. Directions given to students for re-creating Adrien Stoutenburg's "Reel One."

Notes

1. During the past few decades there have been hundreds of articles and dissertations written to explore variables affecting the reader and the reader's response. For information about works written before 1970, see Alan Purves and Richard Beach (1972). For information about works written after 1970, see Richard Beach and Susan Hynds (1990).

2. Probably the first major study of readers' interpretations of texts was I. A. Richards's *Practical Criticism* (1929). Giving sets of poems—with titles and authorship omitted—to college undergraduates from Cambridge University and elsewhere, Richards asked his readers to write freely about the poems. Because Richards had a clear sense of how each text should be interpreted and was little interested in his readers' meaning-making processes, he devoted his efforts to identifying and illustrating students' reading problems: not understanding the plain sense of the work; being unable to interpret its imagery; allowing mnemonic irrelevances, stock responses, doctrinal adhesions, and technical and critical suppositions to blunt their abilities to understand the text. James Squire (1964) and James Wilson (1966) used seven categories to analyze students' interpretations: literary judgment, interpretational, narrational, associational, self-involvement, prescriptive, and miscellaneous. Alan Purves (1968) reduced the major elements of response to four: engagement-involvement, perception, interpretation, and evaluation.

3. During the past decade, several major methods for analyzing readers' readings have been published. Eugene Kintgen (1983) uses twenty-four categories to identify the elementary mental operations that he senses his readers are using: (1) read, (2) select, (3) locate, (4) comment, (5) narrate, (6) phonology, (7) form, (8) word, (9) syntax, (10) tone, (11) paraphrase, (12) deduce, (13) deduce: world, (14) connect: poem, (15) connect: world, (16) connect: literature, (17) connect: figure, (18) generalize, (19) text, (20) justify, (21) restate, (22) illustrate, (23) qualify, and (24) recall. Michael Benton and Geoff Fox (1985) identify four mental activities that readers engage in: (1) picturing, (2) anticipating and retrospecting, (3) interacting, and (4) evaluation. Patrick Dias (1987) identifies four kinds of readers: (1) paraphrasers, (2) thematizers, (3) allegorizers, and (4) problem-solvers. Jack Thomson (1987) identifies six stages of reading: (1) unreflective interest in action, (2) empathizing, (3) analogizing, (4) reflecting on the significance of events and behavior, (5) reviewing the whole work as a construct, and (6) consciously considered relationship with the author, recognition of textual ideology, and understanding of self (identity theme) and of one's own reading processes. Michael Benton et al. (1988) report the results of a couple of classroom-based research studies. In one, English teacher Ray Bell identifies four stages of student response: (1) identification of the individual with the poem, (2) projection of self into the poem, (3) clarification of an emotional response, and (4) intellectual or conscious delight. In a second study, English teacher Keith Hurst hypothesizes that readers perceive a text through three possible frames: (1) seeing the text as story, (2) viewing the text as the product of a creator, and (3) analyzing its form. Judith Langer (1989) hypothesizes that readers use four major stances in the process of understanding a text: (1) being out and stepping into an envisionment, (2) being in and moving through an envisionment, (3) stepping back and rethinking what one knows, and (4) stepping out and objectifying the experience. And Douglas Vipond and Russell Hunt (1989; Vipond et al. 1990) hypothesize that readers choose among three modes of reading: (1) information-driven reading, (2) story-driven reading, and (3) point-driven or dialogic reading—where ". . . readers imagine themselves to be in conversation with authors and texts" (Vipond et al. 1990, 113).

4. Our developing understanding of the concepts of *situating* and *situation* came, in part, from the writings of several sociologists, psychologists, and philosophers. George Herbert Mead's theory of the *social self* ([1934] 1962), Peter Berger and Thomas Luckmann's landmark study of the *social construction of reality* (1966), Michael Polanyi's concept of *personal knowledge* (1958, 1966), Lev Vygotsky's ground-breaking study of the *social foundations of mental development* (1962, 1978), and Jerome Bruner's many explorations into *modes of knowing and thinking* (1965, 1986, 1990) were enormously influential in helping us understand more fully the social and personal dimensions of meaning making. We are also deeply indebted to George Lakoff and Mark Johnson for their pioneering study of *metaphorical language* (1980), to the Russian philosopher and literary theorist Mikhail Bakhtin for his conception of *dialogue* and *voice* (1981, 1984, 1986), and to the British philosopher and historian R. G. Collingwood for his understanding of *history*

and art as situated events ([1938] 1958, [1946] 1956). All of these writers helped us to understand the extent to which our own and others' interpretations of a text are contingent upon our social and personal situations.

II Exploring Students' Readings of Literature

2 Albert and David: Sensing the General Situation

Albert's Readings

1. I thought it was a guy and a girl going to the movies together and then home. (A date more likely.)

2. I thought they were describing the movie and how people react to it.

3. I thought they were describing the movie and how it had a lot of action and when they got outside it was boring and dull.

4. Well I looked for the easy one the first time, and then I read it with a little more detail, and then I read it real carefully and wrote what I thought it was about.

(Eleven-year-old sixth grader)

David's Readings

1. The poem was about a boy taking a girl to a movie and then walking in the snow.
   It was lovely.
   I imagined him to be looking at the refreshing sight of snow and not saying a word, just thinking.

2. He was watching a color movie with lots of blood and fire. Then he left and started walking down Bullet Road to home so many miles away with a girl at his side and her hand in his. The countryside was silent. There was not a whisper to be heard. The snow was falling and it was night.

3. The poem seems boring now after the third time. I noticed all I was going to notice the second time but it does seem to remind me of something now. A few years back in Putnam Valley where I live, I went to a movie with a friend, a double-feature. And by the time we got out, the roads were closed because of snow (there was a couple of feet) and his mom couldn't drive over. So we walked about five

miles to his uncle's house and stayed there for a few days until the storm stopped and we could make it home.

4. I wrote what I wrote because that's what I thought the poem was about. Why I thought what I thought I don't know, but it's probably because that's the way I was raised.

(Eleven-year-old sixth grader)

Our Opening Conversation

Harold: Both Albert and David are writing about a couple going to the movies and then walking home together. They are sensing the outline of what we are calling the *general situation* of "Reel One."

Mark: That sensing seems to be predicated on their having asked, What is this *about*?

Harold: It's true that Albert says, ". . . I thought it was about," and David says, "The poem was about. . . ." But I'm not sure they were asking that question. Maybe they were asking: What's going on here? What's happening? But it came out as *it's about,* because they were writing about a text.

Mark: I think it's significant that they don't start out by saying, "This poem *means*. . . ." Whatever question they were asking, it leads to their summarizing the general situation, indicating who is involved and what is happening.

Harold: Then I believe they are asking, So what? Millions of people go to the movies and walk home afterward. So what is so unusual about this couple, or this movie experience, or this walking home? That's the second question they are trying to answer.

Our Sense of Albert's Readings

Mark: At first Albert summarizes the general situation by bringing the words to life and life to the words. I am assuming that what's *not said* in Albert's first reading is his picking up on certain details. But rather than focusing on the details, he works on his summary of the general situation.

Harold: I must admit that when I chose Albert's readings, I thought they were representative of so many others that said basically, "It's about a couple going to the movies and then home again." But as I look more carefully at what he has written, and as I imagine each situation that his words are so briefly describing, I can see that his readings get more specific over time. In his first reading, he just summarizes the *physical action:* "going to the movies . . . and then home." But in his second reading, he begins to sense the *psychological action:* "they were describing the movie and how people react to it." Then in his third reading, he begins to sense the contrast between the two events and the couple's *specific reaction* to each: "it had a lot of action" and "it was boring." Each time he makes his summary of the general situation more specific.

Mark: You could say he's making each summary more specific, but he doesn't do it by giving us the details that he says he keeps noticing. He's looking at more and more details; but instead of mentioning them, he uses them to *refine* his summary.

Our Sense of David's Readings

Mark: David has a different way of reading. Like Albert, right away in his first sentence he summarizes the general situation to orient himself. But then he *imagines* that general situation, as opposed to refining a summary of it. He jumps in and imagines the general situation, right at the beginning.

Harold: "I imagined him to be looking at the refreshing sight of snow and not saying a word, just thinking." "It was lovely."

Mark: And I sense that he's not just asking, What is happening?— which could lead to a listing of details. Instead, I sense that David is asking, What are they experiencing?

Harold: In his second reading, David writes: "He was watching a color movie with lots of blood and fire. Then he left and started walking down Bullet Road to home so many miles away with a girl at his side and her hand in his. The countryside was silent. There was not a whisper to be heard. The snow was falling and it was night." It's all there in 3-D.

Mark: Rather than ignoring details, he pulls them in, he lives them.

Harold: To use Rosenblatt's metaphor [1978, 48–68], the stream of his own background of experience is flowing along with key words of the text, so that "we walked home" becomes "walking down Bullet Road to home so many miles away"; and "the sound track so dead / you could almost imagine / the trees talking" becomes "The countryside was silent. There was not a whisper to be heard."

Mark: And he senses it is night—perhaps from the line "but there wasn't much blue / in the drifts or corners."

Harold: His second reading is such a vivid and beautiful evocation. As I read it, all sorts of images of quiet winter scenes and walks through lightly falling snow were floating through my mind. And I was sensing how sacred the world seems when fresh snow has covered it white and made everything so pure and crystalline. No wonder David imagines the couple "looking at the refreshing sight of snow and not saying a word, just thinking."

Mark: But why does David think his third reading is boring?

Harold: Where does he say that?

Mark: "The poem seems boring now after the third time."

Harold: I don't think it was his reading that was boring. It's his imagined sense of "Reel One," upon a third reading. He's done what he could do with "Reel One."

Mark: So now the *so what* question emerges for him again. And this time his response to asking *so what* is to recall a related situation. His question seems to be, What does this remind me of?

Harold: He could have said, "I have nothing more to say." We had lots of readers who did that. I think it's great that he's willing to recall this situation and share it, though the situation is tangential to "Reel One." He's not recalling an exciting movie, or a walk home with hand holding.

Mark: He's describing being snowbound.

Harold: And I got to wondering, Why is David sharing this story? I don't think he's doing it just to fill up space, but to share something important. The story suggests, to me anyway, that David is living in a community of close relationships. Even in his second reading when he talks about "Bullet Road," it's down *his* Bullet Road, apparently. And when he can't go to his own home during the snowstorm, he can go to a friend's home. But it's not even a friend's home. It's a friend's uncle's home. What a terrific community of people David can rely on when there is a snowstorm. Somehow that reminds me of his phrase "It was lovely." His whole reading of the world is that it is lovely. I just realized that even when he mentions "blood and fire," somehow the blood and fire disappear. Those are not crucial images for him.

Mark: For David, these details indicate it's a color movie.

Harold: Exactly. So to me that is the meaning of his story.

Mark: I love your interpretation—the idea of David's community. If we had been able to speak to him right after he had written this, we could have asked him what his story means to him, and maybe he could have told us. But in the absence of *his* explanation, I find *your* imagining of his situation very engaging and convincing.

Summary Reflections

Mark: I sense that this is a difficult text for these two young readers. Yet each of these responses is powerful, maybe not even considering the age of the readers. They each begin by asking, in one form or another, What is this about? But then after summarizing the general situation, each asks, So what? And that *so what* leads to different questions and ways of making meaning. With each approach the readers pay a price, but they gain a certain amount of power.

Harold: You can't walk down all roads simultaneously.

Mark: Exactly. Albert seems to be asking, What is *really* happening? To answer that, he works at refining his summary of the general situation. In contrast with Albert, David seems to be asking, What are these people experiencing? And to answer that question, he powerfully imagines the general situation.

Harold: And he also recalls a related situation.

Mark: He seems to have asked, What does that remind me of?

Harold: I think it's crucial here that he keeps the two situations separate. There are some readers who would conflate them, so that his situation would be mixed up with the situation of "Reel One." But except for the inclusion of "Bullet Road," David seems to be imagining the general situation first, and then recalling his own situation, as two separate experiences. Though, of course, his own memories of related situations have contributed to his imagining of the "Reel One" situation.

Mark: I'm wondering if he doesn't get "Bullet Road" from the phrase "from bullets to nurses." If we realize that he had read "Reel One" only twice, turning it over each time, somehow the word *bullet* may have stuck in his mind. And he thinks it's "Bullet Road." So, in fact, that isn't something imported. It is something from the text.

Harold: I hadn't thought of that. Yes, how many roads are called Bullet Road?

Mark: That's from the first stanza. Yet, unlike the vast majority of our readers, he is really preoccupied with the experience of the second stanza. It's as if the movie experience is not the crucial thing.

Harold: If his concern had been with the movies, then he might have concentrated on the first stanza and a related movie experience. But his whole evocation of both "Reel One" and his own experience focuses on walking home in the snow. Perhaps David has had a powerful experience on a country lane and that's why he was drawn to the second stanza.

Mark: Perhaps.

Harold: Identifying these four ways of sensing the situation—summarizing the general situation, refining one's summary of the general situation, imagining the general situation, and recalling a related situation—raises two questions in my mind. Are these approaches the ones these readers always use? And as readers grow older, do they develop the ability to use multiple and interrelated ways of making meaning?

Mark: I think we'll be able to answer those questions when we look at our older readers.

Harold: I hope so. What do you think might be a next step for enabling each of these students to read better?

Mark: We certainly see here that using any approach involves a trade-off of some kind. Using one approach often precludes using another, especially for younger readers. So if Albert is trying to refine his summary of the general situation, he might need to avoid imagining it in detail. And if David is trying to imagine the general situation, it's hard—at the same time—to refine a summary of that situation.

Harold: Maybe the next appropriate step for Albert is to be willing to share the specifics that he probably noted but didn't mention.

Mark: No doubt both Albert and David would profit from discussing how they went about sensing the general situation of "Reel One," and from discussing the relative value of their different approaches. In that way, they'll have greater freedom to choose how they'll make meaning—instead of having to rely on just the one or two approaches that come most naturally.

Harold: That leads me to wonder about when and why readers go beyond sensing the general situation of a text. I agree with you that "Reel One" was probably a difficult text for Albert and David, considering that many of their classmates couldn't even sense its general situation. The fact that Albert and David did as much as they did with "Reel One" is extraordinary. But for the most part I'm not happy when I see readers sensing *only* the general situation of a text. For instance, several years ago I had a student teacher who taught *Romeo and Juliet* as if it were a newspaper headline,

"Teenage Lovers Commit Suicide When Warring Parents Oppose Relationship."

Mark: You mean they didn't read the play?

Harold: Not really. The students were ninth graders reading at about the fourth-grade level. The student teacher thought they would enjoy the play, even if they didn't read it. So basically, she'd show them an act from Zeffirelli's film version, and then they'd discuss its general situation and related topics for a day or two. Then she'd show another act from the film, and they'd discuss its general situation and related topics. And so on.

Mark: Were they aware of the warring relationship between the Capulets and the Montagues? Were they aware of the overall plot?

Harold: Yes. They realized that the two households hated each other, and that Romeo and Juliet were rising above their background situations in loving each other. And they understood that Romeo and Juliet died at the end, and that such a death was horrible and should not have happened. But they left most of the play behind in favor of discussing problems with parents, social violence, teenage suicide, and young love.

Mark: Sounds as if they were engaged in some of the major thematic concerns of the work.

Harold: They were. But they were sensing only the *general* situation of *Romeo and Juliet.*

Mark: Were they sensing the general situation in the manner of someone like David, who has imagined it vividly and feelingly?

Harold: Yes, they were definitely feeling, imagining, and experiencing the general situation of *Romeo and Juliet.*

Mark: And you believed that wasn't enough?

Harold: I felt that after seeing the film they should have looked at the text—not all of it, but portions of it—so that they could explore more fully some of the *particulars* that most concerned them about the play.

Mark: Apparently they did explore some of the particulars that concerned them, but in terms of their own situations.

Harold: I know that they recalled related experiences in the manner that David does, but I'm not sure that they explored or analyzed the *particulars* of those experiences.

Mark: What if they had recalled only related experiences?

Harold: Then I think something would have been lost. The same thing happened when this student teacher had these same pupils read Edwin Arlington Robinson's "Richard Cory." The students might just as well have read only a headline, "Rich Man Kills Himself," for they attended to none of the particulars of the text that was before them. Why did Richard Cory kill himself? Because he was rich and all rich people are unhappy, whereas poor people are happy because they have each other and love.

Mark: That's what the students said?

Harold: That was the discussion of "Richard Cory" on the day I observed this class. It's one thing if students don't have the ability to read an entire Shakespearean play, but reading the sixteen lines of Robinson's text was within their grasp. And because they failed to look at its particulars, they treated Richard Cory stereotypically— as a rich man, not as the particular rich man that Robinson describes. Rosenblatt discusses this: "Much of the mismanagement of personal relationships results from following a stereotyped and automatic reaction to the general outlines of a situation instead of responding to the specific characteristics and changing qualities of that situation" [Rosenblatt (1936) 1976, 105].

Mark: I agree with that. But are you saying that you're opposed to readers ever sensing *only* the general situation?

Harold: I'm not sure. I know that sometimes the general situation may be all that we are able to sense upon a first reading. And some texts don't allow us to go beyond sensing the general situation because there is little of a particular situation to be sensed. And that's okay for outside the classroom. But if we're going to help students learn anything, we may have to help them move beyond the general situation. Yet perhaps we don't. I just have these questions: When is it sufficient to sense only the general situation? When is it not? When and why do readers move beyond a sense of the general situation to a sense of the particular situation? When and how should we promote such a movement?

Mark: Obviously, moving from the general to the particular situation is a gradual process. Both Albert and David move beyond their initial sense of the outline of "Reel One," yet neither arrives at what we might call a sense of the particular situation—though each is on his way.

Harold: But the question remains: When should we be content with allowing readers to remain at the level of just sensing the general situation?

Mark: Trust our students. They'll tell us when to move ahead to the particulars.

Harold: Perhaps. But sometimes we may have to help students walk to where they initially don't want to go.

3 Charlene and Teresa: Accounting for the General Situation

Charlene's Readings

1. ALL technicolor—ALL unreal—yet never impossible. The author of this poem is escaping into the movie but his firm hold on his girlfriend's hand allows reality to persist for him—even in a movie theater. I escape when I'm at a movie, too. To have to leave that existence behind you in the seat makes you sigh and the blinding light of reality stings you in the eyes. It doesn't feel joyful. It feels monotonous, boring. So I run home faster and faster, bolt into my room, slam the door, and BLAST the radio! From one escape to the next.

2. Movies are like life, but better cause ya don't have to be the guy getting riddled with bullets, you feel good sitting there, like Huck Finn on his raft drifting down the Mississippi River, looking at the stars, passive, not interfering with the motions, rhythms of life. A content but temporary arrangement. Absorb it, let the rest of the earth stop still and wait. Time will run out eventually. You will have to cater to the stiffness of your back, the pins and needles in your shins. Half-relieved, half-saddened, I depart from a place that has refuged me from the outside. It's a Black Hole—you're as insignificant as the Tom, Joe, Harry sitting next to you. Everybody let it penetrate cause this is gonna be it for now. Oops, too bad, show's over. Out you go, move on, let the next dreamboat clamor in on and on, an unebbing tide of movie watchers. Back out in the street you want to dance after seeing *Footloose*, you want to cry after *Terms of Endearment*, you want to practice Kung Foo on your little brother after *The Last Dragon*. We are all the good guys—until you get home. That's another Hole, but it is biting, annoying, aggravating, screeching, wailing, not at all unreal. Suddenly you are not a good guy any more. Remember when you broke the spoke on your sister's bike? Well, Mom just found out and is gonna sling your ass any minute. Suddenly I want to see another Black Hole. Postponement, I know. I'll collect the money for the paper

route later, I'll do my calculus homework tomorrow morning, I can get up early in the morning.

That eerie feeling when you get out of the theater, a combination of dread, stillness, ecstasy. The world has awakened to my eyes, I noticed

[Apparently the papers were collected before Charlene could complete her sentence. No fourth part was written.]

(Seventeen-year-old twelfth grader)

Teresa's Readings

1. Everything in the poem has a good, detailed description, which allows a good picture to be created in your mind. The speaker seemed to have been affected by the film, since he compared it to life. He says that his bones whistled, which seems to me that it affected his inside.

2. "It was like life, but better." The description is about guns, wars, blood, and death, though the speaker states that it was like life. Death is a part of everyone's life. Death is not an end; it is rather, a new beginning. It is something that must occur, in order to move a person from one life, to a greater life.

3. The snow can stand for a symbol of death. Snow covers all of the trees, flowers, grass, etc. and freezes, therefore, killing all life. But this life does not go into a greater life; it just ends. Death is a part of every living thing, is always present, and constantly occurring.

4. I re-created "Reel One" into a poem about Death leading to a new and better life. We must all experience death, but we move on to continue our lives, but to be happier, in a world where no problems exist. However, there are living things in nature that die and do not continue their lives. We are lucky, since we have the chance to experience a better life, whereas less fortunate living things do not!!

(Seventeen-year-old twelfth grader)

Our Sense of Charlene's Readings

Mark: I'd like to begin with Charlene's writing, because the experience of re-reading it was an eye-opener for me. I don't recall that it was particularly unusual.

Harold: I always thought it was unusual, though I must admit that the first couple of times I read it, I just had a general sense of how she used movies as an escape. I didn't pay attention to the particulars of her experience.

Mark: Well, maybe *unusual* isn't the correct word. I remember her saying in effect, "Okay, I can relate to this. Movies are an escape, and here's my experience of using movies as an escape." But as I re-read it, I was really listening to what she was saying, and it's amazing how her reading takes on a life of its own. I realized that this is a major argument for having students respond in this way, because you can encourage a kind of reflexive thinking which can help them learn about both the situation of others *and* their own situation. I have a feeling that if Charlene were really to think about what she's saying, it would be eye-opening.

Harold: I sense that her reflecting on her own related situation is her answer to the *so what* question. But I don't think she's asking David's question, What does this remind me of? Instead, after she's summarized the situation by saying, "The author of this poem is escaping into the movie . . . ," I sense that she's asking: Do I do that? How do I do that?

Mark: She claims that "the author . . . is escaping into the movie," yet she acknowledges that "his firm hold on his girlfriend's hand allows reality to persist for him—even in a movie theater." So there's this vague distinction between reality and unreality. You're escaping from reality toward unreality, yet that experience is still infused with reality, because it's a real-life experience. In contrast to this *real* experience of the *unreal* in the movie theater, for Charlene "the blinding light of reality" *isn't* "joyful." It's "monotonous, boring." So the movie experience is really not about unreality versus reality, but about experiencing a heightened reality, which for her is the unreal world of the movie compared with the boredom of everyday life. Then in her second reading she seems to have noted the line "It was like life, but better," which she interprets as "Movies are like life, but better. . . ." And then I sense her asking, How are movies like life, but better?

Harold: Her first answer, primarily from the text, is, ". . . ya don't have to be the guy getting riddled with bullets. . . ."

Mark: But then she starts moving again into *her* experience, getting into *her* state of mind, which she compares to that vivid scene when Huck Finn is on the raft at night, looking at the stars. On that raft you're completely able to escape responsibility and be content and passive, almost in a meditative way. Yet there's a kind of undercurrent of urgency in Charlene's writing here because she knows that this isn't going to last, that sooner or later all of the mundane is going to come back.

Harold: But now the mundane is painful: "You will have to cater to the stiffness of your back, the pins and needles in your shins."

Mark: Then she says that when she leaves the movie theater, she's "half-relieved" and "half-saddened." If there's a stark contrast between the heightened reality of the movies and the mundane of everyday life, why would she be "half-relieved" to leave the movie theater?

Harold: I don't think she's relieved to *leave* the movies. She's half-relieved while *watching* the movies, but only *half*-relieved, because the pains of after-movie life will soon be upon her. And she's *half*-saddened when leaving the theater, not totally saddened, because at least she's had a bit of a respite from the problems of everyday life.

Mark: That makes sense. She says that movies are a "Black Hole" in which one is totally insignificant. Then she imagines an unebbing tide of movie watchers. And we better let this unreal, preferred state of mind penetrate while we have a chance. Then when we leave the theater, we experience this momentary illusion of significance and feeling. But when we get home, "That's another Hole. . . ." So it's almost as if *life is this black hole.* And now it's not the movie versus life, but just plain life. And now reality is no longer monotonous and boring. It's very shrill—it's "biting, annoying, aggravating, screeching, wailing. . . ."

Harold: I agree that Charlene feels that her life is a series of holes, but I sense that the black holes—the movies—are good holes because they blot out painful reality. Home, in contrast, is just "another Hole."

Mark: Then, in place of an escape, she uses the word *postponement,* as if somehow we're trying to defer something, some realization. And it could be as simple as just procrastinating about doing homework. But *postponement* also—in connection with that image of the black hole which keeps coming back to me—takes on more significance than just deferring the paper route.

Harold: I hadn't sensed those possible overtones with *postponement,* but I can see your point. Too many black holes of escape could result in postponing real living indefinitely.

Mark: Then she talks about having "That eerie feeling . . . of dread, stillness, ecstasy" when leaving the theater. I'm not sure how carefully she chose those words, but they're incredible words. In all the responses that we got where people were talking about fantasy versus mundane reality, and the contrast of being in a theater versus going out, these are not words that we saw. We saw the word *stillness,* but not in connection with *dread* and *ecstasy.* I don't usually associate dread with ecstasy. The word *ecstasy* literally means to be beside yourself.

Harold: My sense is that her *ecstasy* and *dread* are related to her *half-relieved* and *half-saddened.* You're "half-relieved" because of the movie's holdover effect on you, which is the *ecstasy.* But you're "half-saddened" because the effect is only temporary. Now you've got to go back to the "Hole" of home where you're no longer the good guy and your ass is going to be in a sling. That's the *dread.* And my sense is that she's not talking about *you* in the sense that it's everyone. "Remember when you broke . . . your sister's bike?" My sense is she's talking about *herself.* She's under a lot of pressure, I would surmise—with her family relationships, schoolwork, job responsibilities, and athletics. So when she notes the phrase "It was like life, but better," she uses it to account for her sense of both "Reel One" and her own situation.

Mark: Definitely. By reflecting on her experience with "Reel One" inductively—by "shaping at the point of utterance," as James Britton would say [1982, 139–45]—she distinguishes between heightened reality and boring reality, between experiences that are peaceful and experiences that are anxiety-ridden. She's able to specify such ambiguous emotions as being both "half-relieved" and "half-saddened." She's able to sense a combination of "dread, stillness, ecstasy."

Harold: She's even aware of *when* she seeks to escape from life's "holes," and of the *ephemeral nature* of the best of life's experiences.

Mark: These are powerful reflections.

Harold: They got me to thinking about whether I ever used movies as an escape or a heightened sense of reality when I was a kid. I think I did in a way. Growing up in the late thirties and forties, during World War II, was a time of worry for me about whether my father would be drafted, whether my uncle George would return home safely, whether the U.S. would be bombed, whether the world would escape from the horrors of Hitler and company. Yet when I went to the movies, the only pictures I recall seeing or wanting to see were Hollywood musicals. Despite World War II, I grew up with this fantasy that falling and remaining in love was as easy as the silver screen made it seem.

Mark: I don't think movies were as much of an escape or a heightened sense of reality for me as were books. When I was a kid, I read all these adventure stories. At first I was just an imaginative member of Tom Swift's gang, coping with the neighborhood. But as I grew older, I traveled to foreign lands, climbed formidable mountains, fought my way through forbidding jungles, survived being shipwrecked, flew impossible missions. These experiences were as real as the movie experiences that Charlene describes. I think Rosenblatt is right when she indicates that it is not accurate to describe the reading of literature as just a vicarious experience [1978, 68]. In many ways these adventures that I took through reading were as real to me as anything else in my life. And in their own way they prepared me for living just as fully as did doing my homework and being on the wrestling team.

Harold: No wonder you've been more adventurous than I have.

Mark: I don't think it's just a matter of the books or movies we happened to have read or seen.

Harold: I agree. The cause-effect relationship is not clear-cut. After all, *why* we saw and read the works we did is as important as their effect on us. But I think it's valuable to reflect on and be a bit reflexive about the relationships between our *movie-reel and book lives* and our *nonmovie-reel and nonbook lives.*

Our Sense of Teresa's Readings

Mark: Teresa begins with a general evaluation of the poem: "Everything in the poem has a good, detailed description, which allows a good picture to be created in your mind." That comment could be said about hundreds of works.

Harold: I have to admit that Teresa's readings were one of the ones that threw me most, at least initially. My first response was that they are a total *misreading* of "Reel One." I think I responded this way because they reminded me of a student, years ago, who interpreted Andrew Marvell's "To His Coy Mistress" as being about the love of Jesus. I wondered then, How did she come up with that interpretation? And I began by asking the same thing about Teresa's readings. But unlike the way I responded years ago, I am now trying to approach these readings respectfully, nonjudgmentally, and empathetically. So as I re-read what Teresa had written, I realized that her first reading is really on the mark when she says, "The speaker seemed to have been affected by the film, since he compared it to life" and ". . . his bones whistled, which seems to me that it affected his inside." So two times she's mentioned that the speaker has been affected by the film, and in each case she's cited different supporting evidence. So in her first reading, I believe that she senses to some degree the speaker's general experience with the film.

Mark: What I sense she's doing in these two statements is explaining the situation. She's not just summarizing that the speaker was affected by the film, nor is she imagining his film experience. She is explaining how the "like life" and "bones whistled" lines support her interpretation.

Harold: I like how you're distinguishing among *summarizing, imagining,* and *explaining.* But she doesn't seem to be satisfied with having realized that the film affected the speaker.

Mark: No. Movies affect lots of people. So what? At this point, I sense she's asking, So what?

Harold: So when she notices "It was like life, but better" at the beginning of her second reading, defines the "It" as "death," and reasons that death is better than life, then she's answering her *so what* question.

Mark: As I see it, Teresa sees "It was like life, but better" as a logical proposition. And she tries to *explain* it with a proposition of her own, "Death is not an end; it is rather, a new beginning." In a sense, Teresa is grasping for an understanding which then becomes the basis for seeing all those other things: "The snow can stand for a symbol of death." It all seems to fit. Seeing that statement as a logical proposition and then explaining it is Teresa's way of making meaning.

Harold: I don't think Teresa would say she sees "It was like life, but better" as a logical proposition. She might see it as a puzzle, though, that needs to be solved.

Mark: Yet if you think of our other readers thus far, the answer to the *so what* question for them was rooted in their *sense of the situation.*

Contrast that with Teresa, who says, "I re-created 'Reel One' into a poem about Death leading to a new and better life." Her poem is *not about a situation*—it is about a logical proposition.

Summary Reflections

Harold: In summary, we might say that both Charlene and Teresa are trying to *account* for the general situation. And for a variety of possible reasons—the pull of a personal concern, the complexity of the imagery, previous training—they do not attend fully to the author's words. Instead, once they note "It was like life, but better," they ask, in effect: How can I use this seemingly explanatory phrase to make greater sense of this poem? And in using the phrase, they each interpret the "It" differently. Charlene interprets the "It" as going to better-than-life movies, and then she reflects on her own related situation. Teresa interprets the "It" as "death" and explains the proposition by saying that life after death is better than life. [*Long pause.*] You know, I've been thinking about this phrase, "It was like life, but better," and wondering just how we might better define it. As you know, Labov, in his research on oral narratives, reports that most narratives have an evaluative component, which he defines as "the means used by the narrator to indicate the point of the narrative, its raison d'être: why it is told, and what the narrator is getting at" [1972, 366]. Personally, I believe that evaluation is a part of every statement that we make. But I'd agree that certain statements seem more evaluative than others. So I'd hypothesize that readers might sense one or more such evaluative phrases in most works. In Archibald MacLeish's "Ars Poetica," for instance, the evaluative phrase for me is "A poem should not mean / But be."

Mark: I know what you mean. I've found that students often interpret *Macbeth* on the basis of "Fair is foul, and foul is fair."

Harold: If one had to pick one phrase to account for the general situation of *Macbeth,* that's probably as good as any. And when I was a student teacher, I taught *Julius Caesar* primarily by focusing on the phrase "The fault . . . is not in our stars, / But in ourselves, that we are underlings." I wouldn't do that today, but at the time I think I found great comfort in having a one-phrase way of wrapping up the play. And I can imagine someone reading *Hamlet* and sensing its being encapsulated in Polonius's advice: "This above all: to thine own self be true."

Mark: Or, "The play's the thing."

Harold: Yes. For any major work, there are many possible key phrases.

Mark: And there are many possible interpretations of any phrase.

Harold: Yes. But the majority of our 288 readers interpreted "It" as *the movies* and said movies were better than life because they are more exciting, more colorful, more vivid, more action-packed.

Mark: But weren't there other reasons why some readers thought movies were better than life?

Harold: Yes. Some readers saw the movies as better because "characters don't have real responsibilities," "you can create what you want in the movies and it is not permanent," and "people in the movies are superhuman—perfect."

Mark: Other readers defined "It" not as the movies but as a special kind of movie.

Harold: Yes. "It must have been the first color movie." "The movie was one of a kind in its time." "They must have gotten a new projector."

Mark: But some readers interpreted "It" as "violence" or "war."

Harold: They explained that violence or war was better than life by saying "the persona was deranged" or "the speaker must be a little crazy" or "the author must like violence."

Mark: So we did have many different interpretations of the phrase "It was like life, but better."

Harold: Yes. But most of our readers, after they had noted and interpreted this evaluative phrase, stopped reading.

Mark: Yet a few students were spurred on by that evaluative phrase to explore more of "Reel One."

Harold: One was the fifteen-year-old boy who interpreted "It" as a war movie and then couldn't understand why the speaker would regard a movie about death as better than life. Then in his final reading, he said: "The only thing I could come up with to explain this poem is the title. In a movie there is more than one reel. This is the same with a person's life. He still has more of a life to live."

Mark: And so it is with our readers. They are still young. They're doing what they can now. And they still have more of their lives to live. It's all right if they just look at one key phrase of the text and use it to account for the rest of the work—if that's all they're able to do at that point in their reading.

Harold: I keep thinking of several beginning teachers who taught

Robert Frost's "The Road Not Taken" as meaning "you should be different and not follow the crowd"—because they focused on only the last two lines: "I took the one less traveled by, / And that has made all the difference." Yet earlier in the text, Frost describes the two roads as "Really about the same." So if the roads are really about the same, then the poem is about the experience of choosing between two different, but equally valid, options and about how the choice will make "all the difference." I find this a much richer reading than seeing the poem as a little sermon about "you should be different from the crowd."

Mark: Is that the way you've always interpreted "The Road Not Taken"?

Harold: No. I think I used to read the poem as that little sermonette that I now find limiting.

Mark: And maybe someday you'll read "The Road Not Taken" as supporting both of these interpretations and being more ambiguous than you now sense it is.

Harold: Perhaps. I guess that I have a tendency to criticize others for being the reader I used to be. It's so hard as a teacher not to want to place students in a hothouse and force them to grow up overnight to my present level of understanding.

Mark: The major struggle throughout my years of teaching has been between wanting to give students all that I know about a work and realizing that if I give it to them, it will be as meaningless as all the stuff that teachers gave me when I didn't ask for it and couldn't understand it. It's so hard to be satisfied with where students are now.

Harold: But I recall thinking years ago that this is perhaps the first and last time they will ever read this work, so I'd better give them all that I know, or they'll never, ever get it.

Mark: And how much of all the knowledge that your teachers gave you has stayed with you?

Harold: It's in my notebooks—or used to be, until I threw them all out—but not in my head. Yet the questions that I keep wrestling with are: When, how, and how much should I intervene in a student's learning? When does a student need my help? What's my role?

Mark: Your way of looking at the situation has shifted from a focus on you and your teaching to a focus on your students and their learning. It shouldn't be a matter of, How much have I got that I want to give to them? Instead, it should be a matter of, Where are they now and how can I help them accomplish what they're trying to do?

Harold: And when and how might I suggest to them additional goals and means?

Mark: In the classroom we're not the sole source of guidance. Students can learn from each other, just as we have.

Harold: But I keep reflecting on what my role is in their learning. So, what might be a next desirable step for each of these readers—besides putting them in a classroom where they can share their readings with other students?

Mark: I believe that if Charlene were to focus primarily on the situation of "Reel One," she would have no difficulty imagining that situation as explicitly as she has imagined her own situation.

Harold: I'd begin by asking her whether she'd prefer to focus on the situation of "Reel One" or her own situation, or both. If she chose her own situation, then I'd encourage her to be, as you suggested, more *reflexive*. She's already described and defined her situation. Now she might profit from *reflecting on her reflecting*, noting patterns in her life and exploring such questions as, What might I do about this? As for Teresa, I find it hard to determine a next step—because I don't know why she is reading as she is.

Mark: She began by explaining the general situation of "Reel One." Perhaps she resorts to treating literature as a logical proposition when she's trying to get a *higher* understanding of a work. If that's the case, I'd show her how she can more fully understand a work by staying with a sense of the situation and exploring it through other approaches.

Harold: But I'd also try not to demean her interpretation. If death has played a recent role in her life, or if she has a strong religious belief in life after death, I'd need to be especially careful.

4 Patrick and Jerome: Sensing the Particular Situation

Patrick's Readings

1. A guy watching a horror film with his girlfriend in winter. He holds her hand as he walks home. Snow is falling. Snow covers everything. It is so silent that you imagine that the trees are talking.

2. A guy is watching a movie, horror, maybe 3-D. Colors to him seem amplified, guns shine brightly, and blood seems redder than usual. Explosion on the screen. He shakes with tension and fright.

He walks home with his girlfriend, holding her hand tightly. It's snowing. The streets hold no shadows, there's only the white of the snow everywhere. The streets are empty. The snow makes no sound as it falls, and muffles their footsteps. All is silent. Their overwrought imaginations make it seem as if the trees are talking to them.

3. A guy is watching a movie, horror, maybe 3-D. Colors seem amplified, guns shine brightly, and blood is redder. Explosion on the screen, he shivers in tension and fright. It all seems so real, but it's better than reality because it can't hurt him.

He walks home with his girlfriend, he holds her hand tightly, no shadows to conceal killers, only the glaring white of the snow. All is absolutely silent, so his overworked imagination makes voices out of the wind in the trees.

4. Each time I read the poem, I saw something new, a little detail here and there, and its significance. All this helped me see more clearly, perhaps, what the author meant to say in the poem. I still don't understand why he chose "Reel One" for the title. Actually, now I do. "Reel One" refers to the movie. See? Another detail found and clarified. This is a very deep poem, with significance on many levels. It was fun analyzing it.

(Fourteen-year-old ninth grader)

Jerome's Readings

1. "The poem is about a man during a war: probably World War II." When I read the first three lines or so, that was what I thought first. "Oh, another poem about a person who was wounded physically and most of all internally." The reading of the second stanza changed what I originally thought, and realizing what the title was, I immediately changed my angle of perception towards the poem.

Although I'm still looking for a better understanding of the poem, I decided the poem to be about a person's emotional shift or wave of thought on a film.

What I then thought about was the movie *Platoon*. It very much resembled what happened to me when I watched the film last weekend. The gun shots, blood, the huge screen, and added to all this was the reality of the Vietnam war, which for the first time was portrayed to me. After the movie it was not snowing, but it was misting a bit. Actually this poem is so much like what I experienced last weekend that it makes me wonder about. . . .

Anyway, this poem is basically broken up into two parts: the first stanza is about what the man saw and felt during the movie and the second stanza concerns the man after the film, walking home with his girl.

One word or part of the second stanza which puzzles me though. Now that I have written this much, I'm not really sure what it said but—Oh it was the two words "sound track" used in the second stanza. I thought that the scene was outside the theater in the second stanza but maybe it isn't. Or maybe "sound track" is just being used as a metaphor.

It seems as though the first stanza is trying to show the power of the war as the film itself and the second stanza is about the silence and thoughts that are going through the man's mind.

I'd like to say that this poem is exactly a piece of literature which pictures what happened to me last weekend, but there must be so much more to it than what I know about the poem.

So much time has passed since I last read the poem that I can't seem to write anything about it. Reels, blood, nurses, sound track, snow . . . so many things are going through my mind now.

2. I, now, doubt or at least question my initial presupposition of the poem. The poem, evidently, has to do with a certain type of art. Well that may be nothing revolutionary, but it's important to always keep in mind.

The particular type of art which I'm beginning to consider is a sketch or painting of a certain scene. The author is always referring to the various colors in both stanzas. I'm really not sure why the author used such metaphors as ". . . guns gleamed like cars" and ". . . red as paint on dancers."

3. Could the word "reel" have a connotation to it? Does it actually mean both reel (a cylinder, spool, or frame that turns on an axis and is used for winding ropes and tapes) and real (not imaginary, fictionalized, or pretended)? If so, what is the "reel one" symbolizing in the poem? Maybe the poem is about a war. However, the second stanza does not represent a type of setting in a war. The colors talked about in the second stanza are white and blue. To me, white and blue represent other words as cold, peace, silence, and serenity. Other words in the stanza are snow, if I recall correctly, silence, and his girlfriend which I interpret as peace. Could all of these be symbolizing heaven?

What am I trying to say? The first stanza could be about what the man saw and experienced during the war, and in fact, the first stanza may be a scene when the man is dying from the wounds.

The second stanza, which is an extensive change, is about the man. It's his death in a type of heaven. Maybe this notion came about by being carried away with my creativeness and imagination, but it's not one that is totally absurd.

One thing I'm constantly reminding myself is about the sudden change in the stanza's setting, tone and pace. The second stanza is much more slower, and peaceful. In contrast, the first stanza includes a sense of action, fast pace, and aggressiveness.

4. It seems as though I just ended my observations with questions. Why did I do this? It's because I'm still so curious about the poem.

I personally think that the most important discovery, or it might have been something reinforced, was that there could be so many interpretations of a piece of literature. One will find out so much about the poem and about the people through the different interpretations.

As a teacher, it will become my job to try to bring out as many interpretations as possible and leave it up to them to choose or even just like one.

(Twenty-year-old college undergraduate)

Our Sense of Patrick's Readings

Mark: I'll admit that when I first read Patrick's readings, I thought they were just unfeeling paraphrases.

Harold: Why did you sense that?

Mark: Maybe because of Patrick's short, declarative sentences, especially in his first reading. It's as if he's reading the text line by line and doing a gloss of each.

Harold: I can see what you mean by his short, declarative sentences: "A guy watching a horror film with his girlfriend in winter. He holds her hand as he walks home. Snow is falling. Snow covers everything." It's a sort of Hemingway prose. But despite Patrick's staccato style, I sensed that he is imagining the situation. The basis of his imagining is his sense, stated at the beginning of his first reading, that the couple saw "a horror film."

Mark: And as he goes through his other readings, it's as if he is thinking recursively: he goes back and repeats phrases and extends them a little. Actually, we could say that Patrick is *deductively* imagining the situation, since he is constantly, as he says, finding and clarifying new details by subsuming them within his initial and explicit sense of the situation.

Harold: In his effort to "see more clearly, perhaps, what the author meant to say," Patrick attends to more of the author's words than do any of the readers we've looked at thus far. Of the two readers in chapter 2, for instance, David uses the author's words the most *explicitly* in sensing the "Reel One" situation. Yet the primary voice is his own. So when David says that the speaker "was watching a color movie with lots of blood and fire," I'd argue that David has focused on only five of the author's thirty-eight words in the first stanza: *technicolor, bullets, blood, screen,* and *fire*. And one of those words, *bullets,* he imports to his imagining of the second-stanza situation.

Mark: Yes, "walking down Bullet Road."

Harold: In his more detailed imagining of the second-stanza situation, however, David uses most of the words from the first four lines ("I held my girl's hand, / in the deepest parts, / and we walked home, after, / with the snow falling") and probably most of the eighth line ("the sound . . . so dead"). So in imagining the situation, David has relied on some of the most vivid words—*technicolor, bullets, blood, fire*—and what I think are the two most syntactically and semantically clear clauses: the first four lines of the second stanza. But in spite of that, he's ignored approximately two-thirds of Stoutenburg's words. In contrast to David, Patrick attends more fully to the author's words, especially the *qualifying* words. "The guns gleamed like cars / and blood was as red / as the paint on dancers" becomes "Colors seem amplified, guns shine brightly, and blood is redder." "The screen shook with fire / and my bones whistled" becomes "Explosion on the screen, he shivers in tension and fright." "I held my girl's hand, / in the deepest parts / . . . but there wasn't much blue / in the drifts or corners" becomes "he holds her hand tightly, no shadows to conceal killers." And "the sound track so dead / you could almost imagine / the trees were talking" becomes "All is absolutely silent, so his overworked imagination makes voices out of the wind in the trees."

Mark: Patrick hasn't just identifed these words in isolation and then tried to interpret them, as I had initially thought. First, as you indicated, he's imagined a situation of a guy watching a horror film with his girlfriend. Then he draws in the author's words to help him flesh out the details within that imagined situation. In the process, he's created this very timid guy at this horror film, clinging to his girl and being overwrought.

Harold: "He shakes with tension and fright." "[H]e holds her hand tightly." "Their overwrought imaginations make it seem as if the trees are talking to them." And on the way home, there are "no shadows to conceal killers."

Mark: Now some readers might say that what Patrick is doing is attending *only* to the author's words and in the process has overcome his own voice and is reading "objectively." But it is his own voice that is the foundation for enabling him to attend to the author's words.

Harold: One could argue, of course, that Patrick's reading is best when it stays closest to paraphrasing or just repeating the author's words, as he does in his first reading. But just doing that doesn't explain *why* "the guns gleamed," "the blood was as red /as," "there wasn't much blue," "you could almost imagine." In order to make sense of the author's qualifying words, Patrick has to imagine a plausible situation that will give those words what Patrick calls "significance." And he does that by imagining the couple experiencing and feeling the after-effects of a horror film.

Mark: That's his answer to his *so what* question. He's trying to sense the significance of each of the author's words. He's asking, What is the significance of each of the details of this situation? He's attending to these particulars to understand a human experience, not to abstract a theme statement. And he determines their significance by *situating* these words, using his own voice as the foundation for listening to the author's words.

Harold: That enables him to make sense of the "like life, but better" line: the movie is better "because it can't hurt you." And he even makes sense of the title: " 'Reel One' refers to the movie."

Mark: He says, "Another detail found and clarified." He liked doing this. "It was fun analyzing it."

Harold: He is analyzing not by summarizing or explaining but by *imagining.* He works *with* the author's words to co-create his sense of the "Reel One" situation.

Our Sense of Jerome's Readings

Mark: Jerome, in contrast with Patrick, does *not* develop a strong sense of the situation.

Harold: That's what I see now. But when I encountered his readings for the first time several years ago, I was completely puzzled. At that time I didn't know how to help him—except to guide him to my interpretation of the text. But, thanks to the new concepts we've been creating over the past nine years, I think I better understand what Jerome is doing. I see that he does not have a strong sense of the "Reel One" situation. I've been thinking about why that happens. In the penultimate paragraph of his first reading, Jerome says, ". . . there must be so much more to it. . . ." And then his last words are "Reels, blood, nurses, sound track, snow . . . so many things are going through my mind now." He's got all these words rotating around, each sort of a magnet pulling him in a different direction. And he has this belief that there's got to be so much more. There's got to be symbolism and depth.

Mark: It's his answer to the *so what* question. Although his experience with the movie *Platoon* suggests an almost uncanny resemblance to the situation he senses as he reads "Reel One," Jerome disregards this as a possible basis for making meaning and proceeds with other ways of dealing with the author's words.

Harold: As I see it, in dealing with the author's words, Jerome goes through four different interpretations. His first one, which he mentions in the first two lines, is that it's "about a man during a war: probably World War II." And that he rejects for two reasons— the second stanza and the title don't fit. Then he senses that "Reel

One" is about going to a movie similar to the one he saw, *Platoon,* and walking home afterward.

Mark: And in the process, he begins reflecting on his own movie experience and vividly imagining it. But he cuts himself off.

Harold: Because he feels that he has to get back to the text. Yet he does sense a contrast between the first and second stanzas, with the first "trying to show the power of the war" as a film and the second about "the silence and thoughts" after the film.

Mark: But when talking about the text, he is not *imagining* this contrast so much as *explaining* it: "this poem is . . . broken up into two parts . . ." and "the first stanza is trying to show. . . ."

Harold: But he's not content with that because he believes "there must be so much more to it. . . ." So at the beginning of his second reading, he comes up with a third interpretation: "The poem, evidently, has to do with a certain type of art." He indicates that the colors and comparisons—"guns . . . like cars" and "paint on dancers"—caught his attention.

Mark: Perhaps he has in mind a pop art painting.

Harold: Possibly. But after exploring possible meanings of "reel" at the beginning of his third reading, he concludes, "Maybe the poem is about a war." So his fourth interpretation returns to his first, even though he had initially rejected that for two good reasons. This time, however, he makes the second stanza fit by interpreting it as "his death in a type of heaven."

Mark: He comes closest, I think, to imagining a situation in what you call his second intepretation, in which he says, ". . . I decided the poem to be about a person's emotional shift or wave of thought on a film." But this still leaves him asking the *so what* question.

Harold: He found his movie experience with *Platoon* so similar to his experience of reading "Reel One." Yet he believes his own, similar experience is not relevant as he tries to make meaning of "Reel One."

Mark: It's as if Jerome is attempting to listen to the author's words— without listening to his own voice. He feels that it is his responsibility to attend to the words on the page and consider what they might add up to. And since this is *literature,* they ought to add up to something that matters: a statement about war or art or life and death.

Harold: Some big theme like that. He says he discovered or had reinforced the idea that a piece of literature can have "so many interpretations."

Mark: When you approach reading as placing the author's words in as many different *contexts* of significance as possible, the number of possible interpretations is almost infinite. It's no wonder that he concludes, "As a teacher, it will become my job to try to bring out as many interpretations as possible and leave it up to them [the students] to choose or even just like one."

Harold: He places the colors and descriptions in the context of "a certain type of art." Then he interprets "white and blue" in isolation and asks: "Could all of these be symbolizing heaven?"

Mark: He observes that maybe he does get "carried away" with his "creativeness and imagination." What he's doing is creative and imaginative in one way, but he's not engaged in experiencing the author's words as aspects of a richly imagined situation.

Summary Reflections

Mark: In summary, we see here the difference between attending to the author's words within an imagined sense of the situation and moving images about to see what sort of contexts might give them significance.

Harold: Jerome's interpreting "white" and "blue" and "snow" as "heaven" reminds me of so many of our young readers who did similar things.

Mark: I remember one college reader who identified the isolated colors "red," "white," and "blue" and concluded "Reel One" was about patriotism!

Harold: There's a problem, then, when readers seek to find *contexts* for words instead of sensing a situation in which the words could have meaning. But can we explain just what the difference is between *seeking a context* and *sensing a situation*? Is it just a matter of taking into account more of the words on the page?

Mark: That's part of it. But, more importantly, *being situated is being aware of the meaning makers involved.* And the meaning makers include, among others, the author or authors, the various persons or characters whose voices the author includes in the situation, and the reader or readers who are sensing and making sense of the author and the characters' situations. When Jerome says, ". . . I decided the poem to be about a person's emotional shift or wave of thought on a film," and then says, "What I then thought about was the movie *Platoon*," he is sensing both the speaker's possible situation and his own related situation. But when he says, "The poem, evidently, has to do with a certain type of art," he is placing words in a context by ignoring both the speaker and his own situation.

Harold: But when he explains that the first stanza is "about what the man saw and experienced during the war" and the second stanza is about "his death in a type of heaven," isn't he sensing what he thinks might be the speaker's situation, and not just a context?

Mark: It's true that in this meaning making Jerome is more attentive to the speaker than he is in his "certain type of art" interpretation. But he's still ignoring *himself* in the meaning making, which is why I'd say that even this is a *contextualized*, and not a *situated*, interpretation.

Harold: How do you sense that he's ignored himself?

Mark: Jerome says, "Maybe this notion came about by being carried away. . . ." He's aware that this interpretation does not really match *his* sense of the "Reel One" situation: "a person's emotional shift or wave of thought on a film." But he rejects that *situated* interpretation because he believes "there must be so much more to it. . . ."

Harold: I think I have a sense of what Jerome is doing here. Recently I saw an off-Broadway production of Harold Pinter's *The Homecoming*. I had never read the play or seen a production of it, but I had seen a couple of Pinter's other plays. So I expected the dialogue to be sparse—with few explanations and lots of gaps for the viewer to fill.

Mark: Were your expectations realized?

Harold: Yes, but more so than I believe they should have been. I left the theater, feeling like one of the young readers in our research, wondering if I understood much of anything about what had happened.

Mark: You didn't have any sense of the situation?

Harold: In summary form the play made sense, but I had difficulty interpreting the particulars. I felt something was missing. So I began wondering whether I was to take the play realistically—as about a family in North London—or allegorically or metaphorically. Yet the setting was realistic, as was much of the acting. So I concluded that the problem must be in the directing. And as I left the theater, I heard others discussing what the play was about. One man explained to the woman beside him that it was really about the Thatcher administration, and someone else thought it was about Soviet-American relationships. And had I been younger, I might have jettisoned my general sense of *The Homecoming* situation in favor of reading it metaphorically or allegorically.

Mark: In other words, you might have given it a *contextualized* interpretation.

Harold: That's my point. It would have been so easy to do what I sense Jerome did here and what I sensed some other members of the theater audience were doing. If I couldn't give Pinter's *The Homecoming* an adequate *situated* interpretation, why not forget about my primary sense of what was happening and choose some context to give it meaning? But I didn't succumb to that impulse. And I'm glad I didn't, because the following day the *New York Times* reviewer commented that aspects of the production's directing and acting were so blunted that it was difficult, if not impossible, to sense the power and significance of *The Homecoming.*

Mark: You were vindicated.

Harold: And I was so grateful to realize that I was not at fault as a reader. But as a result of reflecting on this experience now, I feel I can be more understanding of Jerome's desire to want "Reel One" to be more than he sensed it could be when he gave it a *situated* interpretation.

Mark: Unfortunately, he never gave it much of a situated interpretation. He cuts himself off when he says, "Actually this poem is so much like what I experienced last weekend that it makes me wonder about. . . ."

Harold: What if he had completed that sentence by using his analytic skills to explore the relationship between his experiences with *Platoon* and his sense of the "Reel One" situation as "about a person's emotional shift or wave of thought on a film"?

Mark: If he had done that, I don't think Jerome would be asking, So what? I think the next desirable step for Jerome might be to go back to where he cut himself off.

Harold: Perhaps. But I sense that Jerome might profit more from learning the difference between a contextualized reading and a situated reading—between placing the author's words into various contexts and sensing the particular situation.

Mark: As for Patrick, I think his reading is as complete as it can be. Yet he might profit from hearing how other readers sensed the particular situation of "Reel One," how it could be viewed as something besides a *horror film* experience.

Harold: Your suggestion that Patrick hear how other readers sensed the particular situation of "Reel One"—and I agree that would be valuable—raises a question in my mind: What does it mean to sense the particular situation, and how much of the particular situation does a reader have to attend to? For instance, I had a student teacher a few years ago who took *three months* to have her pupils read *To Kill a Mockingbird.* They interpreted almost every line.

Mark: We'll be dealing with this issue in part three of this book. But for now I'd say that sensing the particular situation is not primarily a matter of accumulating details about every aspect of plot, every description of setting and character, every use of language.

Harold: I think the problem arises when teachers approach a work *chronologically* rather than *conceptually.* Interpreting a text is a matter of sensing one or more of the major issues and then exploring the particulars related to those overall concerns.

Mark: Otherwise the work becomes a mass of trivia without a center around which the particulars can be organized and given meaning.

Harold: Patrick, I believe, demonstrates the process of meaning making quite nicely. He is moving through the text and adding one detail to the next. But what enables the details to cohere is Patrick's overall conceptual sense of the situation: "A guy watching a horror film with his girlfriend. . . ." And his ability to add more and more particulars upon each re-reading is not so much a matter of his reading chronologically, but of his reading recursively. His reading, discovering, and learning is more spiral than linear. Of course, he didn't have the text to look at when he was writing.

Mark: Even if he had, his understanding of it still would have been recursive rather than linear, which illustrates, as do all our readings, that readers need to re-read texts in order to make sense of them more fully.

Harold: If only I had had the opportunity to read literature that way when I was in school—instead of having to remember and make sense of all the particulars of a text upon a first and only reading!

5 Nick and Vanna: Accounting for the Particular Situation

Nick's Readings

1. I think the poem was written from the point of view of an ignorant person who has been sensually dulled by television and its bigger-than-life panorama. Walking with his girlfriend in a love relationship—which should be the most sensual of all experiences—he finds lacking compared to the tube.

2. He sees a kind of artistic (forgive me for using that word) beauty in the violent images on the TV, while the images of the snow and the trees seem to be boring. Thoughts of nurses—the perfect comforters of TV illusion. Thoughts of nice, shiny guns like nice, shiny cars. Blood so colorful and like the make-up, the gay falseness, on a dancer's face. Beautiful images of bad things and drab images of love, peace, quiet, beautiful things.

3. TV moves him, shakes his bones. Love, sex, his girlfriend—only the trees are talking on the way home.

4. In the three steps I went from a broad overview, to details, to the essence (which is in a sense an overview).

In the first I only wrote what I thought the punchline or the "meaning" of the poem was—there was too much imagery to go into detail.

In the second, I tried to support my first impressions by looking at the details, seeing what they meant and making them add up. This is where I disregarded certain lines because I wasn't sure if they fit my idea, especially the last line—it seemed to be too nice for what I thought was a drab scene.

In the third, I double-checked the ambiguous lines and made them fit. It then all added up and I had the absolute key to this poem, total understanding and divine wisdom. Of course, that is ridiculous, but I had to try anyway.

(Eighteen-year-old twelfth grader)

Vanna's Readings

1. I'm going to think this one through on paper. My first impression is that the speaker is feeling a kind of letdown after leaving the movie theater. At the movie, where he has found an exciting escape, he is drowned in "technicolor"—the blood is really red "as the paint on dancers." This line is particularly vivid for me. Associating the paint with those on dancers conjures up images of African dancers painted with war paint, dancing exotically around a blazing fire to the sound of drums—very vivid. This makes the paint glisten and become warm in my mind's eye as it mixes with the sweat on the dancers' bodies. There is also a great deal of sound in the first stanza. I hear bullets, crackling fires, drums, dancers, "whistling bones," and cars. Cars screech and the scene is so "real" for the speaker that his own bones "whistle" as do ours.

2. The words "Reel One" suggest the metaphor between a movie "reel" and "real life"—the question being: which one is more real?

In the second stanza the snow is only white—it isn't the icy blue-white snow one finds in the movies, and "the soundtrack so dead" is obviously the movie play on words again. The speaker seems bored by the "white-noise" feeling he finds in real life. He's coming down from the movie-theater high—he's in a kind of withdrawal period. But then something wonderful happens—the greatest movie theater of all begins to come into play. The human imagination begins to work in the midst of all the white noise. The speaker begins to imagine the trees are talking. "Imagine" is the key word here because imagination is the built-in movie of every man. The word "imagine" is for this reason set at the end of a line of the poem, causing us to pause and extend the sound of the word and emphasize its effect.

The speaker concludes at the end of the first stanza that the movie "was like life, but better," but by the final lines of the poem we are wondering what his new feelings are as he imagines that the trees were talking. The speaker realizes or maybe he doesn't that his imagination is where he can find the technicolor he seeks to color his white-on-white world.

3. The lines "I held my girl's hand, in the deepest parts" are also interesting. They are ambiguous because the speaker could mean the deepest parts of the movie and the deepest parts of the snow as well.

The poem suggests or builds a sort of ring in itself. The words "from bullets to nurses" suggest this aspect. Bullets kill, nurses heal—

"technicolor"—these are all-encompassing suggestions. You could begin reading the poem again after the last sentence and attribute the first stanza to the boy's imagination—making sort of a loop—reading and subsequently suggesting the imagination to be "like life, but better" rather than a movie. So the question becomes: just which "reel" are we playing here anyway? The reel of a movie or the reel of the speaker's imagination?

[No fourth part was written.]

(Twenty-three-year-old college graduate student)

Our Sense of Nick's Readings

Mark: I found myself thinking more about Nick's description of what he was doing than about what he actually wrote. He views the reading process as three steps: providing an overview, examining details, and presenting an essence, which he says is another kind of overview.

Harold: He begins with the overview: "I think the poem was written from the point of view of an ignorant person who has been sensually dulled by television and its bigger-than-life panorama." That is his thesis statement.

Mark: And I believe it's his answer to his *so what* question: So, what is the overall meaning of this poem?

Harold: He seems to have arrived at this thesis statement, in part, by not liking what he senses is happening in the second half of "Reel One": "Walking with his girlfriend in a love relationship—which should be the most sensual of all experiences—he finds lacking compared to the tube."

Mark: Then in his second reading he tries to support what you're calling his thesis statement by noting certain details and "making them add up." He's working *deductively.*

Harold: He's trying to work deductively, but it's not as neat as he tries to make it. For instance, he refers to the particular imagery of "The guns gleamed like cars / and blood was as red / as the paint on dancers" when he writes: "Thoughts of nice, shiny guns like nice, shiny cars. Blood so colorful and like the make-up, the gay falseness, on a dancer's face." Nick's interpretation of these lines supports the statement with which he begins his second reading: "He sees a kind of artistic . . . beauty in the violent images on the TV. . . ."

But this second-reading statement about the speaker's sensing "a kind of artistic . . . beauty" is making a different claim, I believe, than his opening thesis about the speaker being "sensually dulled by television."

Mark: Nick's claiming that the speaker is sensually dulled when walking with his girlfriend.

Harold: But his method of writing *deductively* does not allow him to revise his opening thesis statement when he encounters data that doesn't quite fit.

Mark: He's aware that he is doing that. He admits, ". . . I disregarded certain lines because I wasn't sure if they fit my idea, especially the last line—it seemed to be too nice for what I thought was a drab scene."

Harold: And "you could almost imagine / the trees were talking" doesn't support his thesis. I can think of other lines, also, that don't "fit."

Mark: In his reflections, he puts *meaning* in quotation marks. He knows he hasn't been able to make it all fit.

Harold: As he says, ". . . there was too much imagery to go into detail."

Mark: Nick is being ironic when he says, "It then all added up and I had the absolute key to this poem, total understanding and divine wisdom." His understanding of reading makes it ridiculous for him to claim that he's achieved some sort of ultimate interpretation.

Harold: I sense that he's being ironic about the fact that *no one* can.

Mark: No one has "divine wisdom."

Harold: So Nick's way of *deductively explaining* the situation doesn't allow him to assimilate or accommodate to details that don't fit. In contrast, Patrick's way of *deductively imagining* the situation allows him to assimilate more of the author's words and continually co-create new meanings in the process.

Mark: Because Patrick's way of *deductively imagining* the situation is less confining than Nick's way of *deductively explaining* it.

Harold: "A guy watching a horror film" allows more breathing room than "an ignorant person who has been sensually dulled."

Our Sense of Vanna's Readings

Mark: Unlike Nick, Vanna approaches "Reel One" *inductively,* by writing to learn. Although she begins with a summary of her overall sense of the situation, she stipulates that it's her "first impression" and then lets her thoughts go wherever they will as she writes. She seems to be asking: What sense can I make of this by writing to explore and discover?

Harold: She's reading *inductively:* "I'm going to think this one through on paper." And she's not just explaining, as is Nick. She's also *imagining.* When she attends to the author's words "blood was as red / as the paint on dancers," she associates those words with "African dancers painted with war paint," which leads her to imagine "a blazing fire," "the sound of drums," and "sweat on the dancers' bodies." In addition, these images and others lead her to hear "a great deal of sound": "bullets, crackling fires, drums, dancers, 'whistling bones,' and cars." Most of our readers heard *no* sounds in the first stanza; Vanna hears a cacophony. Vanna is so taken by the first-stanza situation that she doesn't go beyond it during her first reading.

Mark: Then, while the vast majority of our readers focused on the line "It was like life, but better," as apparently Vanna did in her first reading, her second reading springs from thinking about the question that the title raises in her mind, Which is more real?

Harold: But she doesn't stay with that, any more than she stayed with the rich imagery of the first stanza, which was so much a part of the basis of Nick's interpretation. My sense is that Vanna's *so what* question is, Where is the key that will unlock the meaning of this poem? Searching for an answer, she continues to explore, attending next to the snow's not being the "icy blue-white snow" of the movies, and then to "the sound track so dead." "But then something wonderful happens," Vanna says, and it's at this point that Vanna finds her key. " 'Imagine' is the key word here because imagination is the built-in movie of every man."

Mark: She's finally articulating her thesis statement.

Harold: To her credit, Vanna doesn't stop here either. Writing inductively allows her, unlike Nick, to revise her interpretations. At the beginning of her first reading, she sensed that "the speaker is feeling kind of let down after leaving the movie theater." But now she senses, "The speaker begins to imagine the trees are talking." So at the end of her second reading, Vanna concludes, "The speaker realizes or maybe he doesn't that his imagination is where he can find the technicolor he seeks to color his white-on-white world." And she doesn't force her insight on the speaker: maybe he does and maybe he doesn't realize the power of his imagination.

Mark: Then, in her final reading, she writes, "The poem suggests or builds a sort of ring in itself." I sense that she's got a delicate balance going here. On the one hand, one might say that she's being tendentious and trying to bend the poem into one whole idea about reeling around and which is the real reel— "The reel of a movie or the reel of the speaker's imagination?" On the other hand, she is listening to the author's words.

Harold: At this point she's interrelating all three of her key phrases: "It was like life, but better"; "Reel One"; and "imagine / the trees were talking." By arguing that you could make "sort of a loop" and begin reading the first stanza after having read the second, she transforms the "It" of "It was like life, but better" into "the imagination." Then she goes beyond all those readers who interpreted "Reel One" as asking a question about the reality of movies versus the reality of life. To her the question is, Which reel is the real reel, the movie or the speaker's imagination?

Mark: This is certainly one of the most imaginative readings, appropriately, that we've had of "Reel One"!

Harold: And just as Vanna doesn't see the stanzas as having to be read in only one direction, she doesn't see the author's words as having only one meaning. She senses *multiple meanings* for "reel"; "the sound track so dead"; "I held my girl's hand, / in the deepest parts." And she doesn't try to close down her reading. At the very end she leaves her key question open. So Vanna gives us a vivid example of *inductively imagining and explaining the situation.* Certainly this is a powerful way of making meaning.

Summary Reflections

Mark: In summary, we could say that these two readers are not only attending to most of the author's words, but they are asking, Why is the author talking about the situation in this way?

Harold: They are not content with just sensing the situation as involving a guy and his girl reacting to a movie, be it an exciting movie, a horror movie, a murder movie, or a war movie.

Mark: The focus is no longer just on sensing the details of a particular human situation, but on constructing a psychosocial explanation to *account* for those details.

Harold: For Nick, it's the power of television to dull the imagination.

And for Vanna, it's the power of the imagination to make all aspects of life more real.

Mark: Yet neither reader overgeneralizes. Each keeps the focus on the "Reel One" situation.

Harold: Nick doesn't say, "I think this poem is about television and how it dulls all of us." He keeps the focus on "the point of view of an ignorant person." And Vanna doesn't say, "We realize or maybe we don't that our imaginations. . . ." She stays with the "Reel One" speaker: "The speaker realizes or maybe he doesn't. . . ."

Mark: A second feature of these readings, I sense, is that each reader believes that it is *the author* who determines meaning and places keys to that meaning in the text. And if the reader is attentive to those keys, the reader can unlock the meaning contained in the text. These readers, I sense, are operating with these *container* and *key* metaphors of reading. For instance, Nick begins, "I think the poem was written from the point of view of an ignorant person. . . ." For Nick, the key is to determine the point of view from which the author has chosen to tell the story, and Nick thinks he's identified that key. For Vanna, the key is the word *imagine*. Of the two readers, she is the more forthright in attributing her interpretation to the author: "The word 'imagine' is for this reason set at the end of a line of the poem, causing us to pause and extend the sound of the word and emphasize its effect."

Harold: But that "end of a line" reasoning could be used to justify emphasizing seventeen other words as well!

Mark: So true! Later Vanna says, "The poem suggests or builds a sort of ring in itself." And, of course, it is the author who creates the poem that "suggests."

Harold: I sense that a third and related aspect of these readings, especially for Nick, is the sense of being slightly overwhelmed by all of the author's words and by trying to interpret their meanings accurately.

Mark: Nick has this sense that his own voice is a potential source of distortion. And Nick and Vanna do not realize that their own voices *are contributing* and *necessarily must contribute* to how they are sensing the situation.

Harold: If we are going to allow or encourage readers to go from sensing the particulars of a situation to some sort of more abstract accounting of that situation, should we allow them to use their own voices, their own meaning-making constructs, or should we give them meaning-making concepts and structures with which to interpret a text?

Mark: I don't think the movement is from one of no accounting of a situation to a full accounting of it. It's a gradual process, and a never-ending process. Patrick, for instance, accounts for the particulars of the "Reel One" situation by saying that the couple is responding to the effects of a horror film.

Harold: That's a *concrete* accounting.

Mark: I suppose you could argue that *horror film* is more concrete than *the imagination*. But the concept of *horror film* is also more abstract than the concept of *popcorn*.

Harold: So when we say that Nick and Vanna are accounting for their own sense of the particular situation, it's not that Patrick and Jerome have not, but only that Nick and Vanna are doing so in a relatively more abstract or theoretical way.

Mark: Of course, one could use even less commonly understood ways of accounting for the particulars of "Reel One" than the ones Nick and Vanna use. I can imagine a critic citing some psychologist's theory of adolescent development as the basis for interpreting "Reel One," or applying some principles of deconstruction as the basis for arguing that "Reel One" has no definite meaning.

Harold: What I'm asking, then, is: At what point should readers be introduced to and asked to use somebody else's psychosocial, economic, political, historical, philosophical, religious, or literary concepts or theory as the basis for their meaning making? For instance, when I began teaching, I often gave students the schema or structure with which I wanted them to read the text. So when I taught Sophocles' *Oedipus Rex,* I began by introducing students to Aristotle's theory of tragedy. And before I had students read Jack London's "To Build a Fire" or Stephen Crane's "The Blue Hotel," I gave a lecture on naturalism and how it differs from realism and romanticism. And before we read Hawthorne's *The Scarlet Letter* or Arthur Miller's *The Crucible,* I lectured on Puritanism. I gave students these institutionally approved meaning-making systems because I thought that texts were the products of and were created to illustrate key concepts, and that students could not make sense of a text unless they had the appropriate lens.

Mark: Did Sophocles, Euripides, and Aeschylus write tragedies to illustrate Aristotle's theory, or did Aristotle create his theory as a way of trying to account for what he sensed was similar about and involved in experiencing these plays?

Harold: Of course, the theorized accounting usually comes afterward. But after the theory has been created, it can then influence the creation of other particular texts.

Mark: But if subsequent texts are to have individual worth, the writer usually modifies or even works against the established theory.

Harold: I guess that's why I abandoned the practice of giving students a priori meaning-making structures. I sensed it was too limiting, too inhibiting. When I was working on my doctorate, for instance, I took a course in the British novel; and one of the texts we were to read was Joyce's *Ulysses*. To prepare us for the reading, the professor gave us a two-hour lecture on what each of the chapters represented and how Joyce was drawing parallels between his characters and related ones from Greek and Biblical literature. This professor's analysis made Joyce's *Ulysses* seem like such a structured and dull creation to me that I did not read it. Since I sensed the text was just a network of allusions all laid out in a one-day structure, and since I knew what the allusions and structure were, I saw no reason for reading *Ulysses*. And when I was able to pass the exam on the book and pass the course—both with an A—my earlier beliefs about not needing to read the text were confirmed.

Mark: Suppose your teacher had asked you and the other members of the class to make sense of the first couple of pages of *Ulysses*— without giving you any structure or concepts, except to ask, "What do you sense is going on here?"

Harold: Asking us to explore the text *inductively*?

Mark: Yes. And then suppose that he had encouraged you to read the rest of the novel as best you could and as rapidly as you could— without worrying about all the things that you might not understand, but focusing on enjoying as much of the characters and their situations as possible?

Harold: I would have read *Ulysses*, enjoying the challenge of trying to make sense of it, and experiencing much of the life of Leopold Bloom. And that's the way I now introduce texts to my students, and the way I read texts. But when, if at all, is it appropriate to introduce students to those more institutionalized concepts, structures, and theories for making meaning?

Mark: After they've shared the results from using their own ways of making meaning. With high school students, however, I've found that their own readings of a text are usually so rich that I don't have to introduce other ways of interpreting the work. But I do so, occasionally, so they'll be aware of other ways of making meaning. But now I do that only after students have made sense of the text, using their own ways.

Harold: The other issue that the readings in this chapter bring to mind, and this is related to the issue we've just discussed, is the question of *deductive* writing. As we know, many English teachers have students write papers in which they are to state and support a thesis about the text they have read.

Mark: They are asked to demonstrate their understanding of a work by stating and supporting a proposition about it.

Harold: And although they may not call it a *proposition,* but a *thesis* or *theme statement,* your use of the word *proposition* suggests that maybe we have students do this because we want our area of study to seem scholarly in the way that mathematics and science are.

Mark: Or maybe we do this because that is the primary way we were taught to write about literature.

Harold: But what happens when we have students write these thesis papers? If we have students write about something that we have discussed in class, most of the papers sound like products from an assembly line. They demonstrate only that students are good parrots. And reading such papers is boring. If, on the other hand, we ask students to write about an aspect of the text that was not discussed in class, most students cannot do this.

Mark: Because they have not been taught how to do this, and they can't do it using a *deductive* format.

Harold: Exactly. If you're going to write about something you haven't yet thought about, you need time and a way to raise questions and explore possible answers to them.

Mark: In other words, you need to learn how to write *inductively.*

Harold: Or work with others, collaboratively in groups, to explore the questions and issues that you have raised.

Mark: Yes, as we have been doing in these conversations.

Harold: In the manner of the *essay,* which means to essay, to try, to explore and discover insights en route.

Mark: In contrast to the *thesis paper,* which requires that you have and state all your insights at the beginning.

Harold: Throughout high school and college, I hated writing those thesis papers because I was basically just stating and supporting some ideas I already had, which I found boring, and because I did not know how to discover new ideas, except by reading what some critics had to say.

Mark: How did you learn to write *inductively,* in the form you're calling the essay?

Harold: I suppose I learned it ten to fifteen years ago from the writings of James Britton and others, as well as from participating in and experiencing the heuristic firsthand in our Oxford Study-Abroad Program. But this was some time after I had completed my doctorate.

Mark: So how do you make sense of texts now?

Harold: By inductively talking to learn, as we are doing now. And by inductively writing to learn, as Vanna does during her readings of "Reel One." When I really want to think through something I've read and to discover as much as I can about it, I write inductively to explore, imagine, and explain the situation. And, in contrast to thesis writing, I love this inductive, essay writing.

Mark: I think I'm still conditioned too much by the old, deductive, thesis-type writing.

Harold: I even explore my dreams and relationships with others through writing to learn. It's terrific. You really learn to carry on a dialogue with yourself, and it's amazing how much you can discover in the process.

Mark: Perhaps a desirable next step for Nick might be to learn how to write inductively. And perhaps a next step for both Nick and Vanna would be to help them realize more fully their own contributions to the meaning-making process.

Harold: Yes. Nick could explore his beliefs about the influence of television, and Vanna could reflect on her own experiences with the imagination. Thus they could realize that they are probably using a personally meaningful concept or theory—one from among a variety of others—to account for the particulars of "Reel One."

Mark: And it would be helpful if they could learn to attend—over time—to increasingly more voices in the situation.

6 Nicole and Jo Ann: Sensing the Voices of the Situation

Nicole's Readings

1. He's comparing his life to a movie. The movie is more interesting, has more "color." In the last sentence in the first paragraph "it was like life, but better." The movie is his fantasy world. It is much better, more is happening, everything seems so life-like that life itself seems drab and boring, sort of colorless.

2. Maybe he had a fight with his girlfriend. "He held her hand in the deepest part" like he was searching for something that really wasn't there at all or maybe never was. The snow was white with no blue. It sounds like his world is totally empty and he is searching for something or someone as he looks for the non-existent blue tint to the snow. It just isn't there and neither are the things he's looking for from his life. He described the movie as being technicolor, full of "life," "everything from bullets to nurses," a comparison to things that happen in ordinary life from muggings, shootings, and being in hospitals. He describes it as though these things don't exist in his world.

3. "The soundtrack was dead"—he and his girlfriend have nothing in common to share, nothing to talk about. The "trees" could have done more talking than he did. He wants to be part of the movie, he wants to live it. Anything, fantasies will be better than his life. He's a dreamer who is uninterested in reality. Life holds no real meaning for him. He wants to escape into something more exciting. He is too immature or insane to handle the real world, so he makes up one that suits his needs. He is only content in his dreams. The title, itself, explains part of the "Reel One." It's a play on words—*reel* as in movie reel and *real* as in reality, true to life. He picks *reel* over *real*. I think he's lonely.

4. I went about this by analyzing words with double meanings. Comparisons of life and fantasy. Trying to picture words as they were

written and thoughts behind the words, feelings of depression or loneliness that might occur in people's lives.

(Fourteen-year-old ninth grader)

Jo Ann's Readings

1. It seems to me that it's about a boy who's watching this movie. In it he feels great excitement like he's part of it and everything's so life-like and real. Maybe he's comparing the dreary snow and life to not everything that's seen on TV or movies is not always like that of real life. It's almost like too sudden a change for him, and it's so different in real life that it almost doesn't seem real—like trees that talk and everything white. He's watching a movie with his girlfriend. In the movie, the life, noise, and color seem to stand out. Maybe he feels his life isn't like that, but he wishes it were when he says it's like I'm there or something like that.

2. Now it looks like it's about a boy watching a war movie and it's almost like he's there, all in color, the guns like cars, the nurses and fighters, the dancers with their paint—almost if it's war. Soldiers against Indians, but he says it's like life—only better. Maybe he has a love for war. But then he steps outside. The dreary snow, everything quiet and white. Sound track is dead, almost like trees talking could refer to maybe now that the movie's gone all reality comes to him. Look at what's happened. War comes and goes, leaves nothing—all stillness. It's like if he's imagining himself in the midst of the afterpast. After the war is over, after the excitement and color have gone and been used up, he sees himself in a lonely place, full of stillness—like him and *his* girl are the only ones left. The snow's falling and the only sounds left are the trees that almost seem to be talking to him or to everyone that this is what happens. Maybe he has this dream after the movie. Maybe he's daydreaming after having gone to the movies. He's trying to picture himself in the future or maybe in the past—how the people in the movie would've felt. The contrast from the movie and the outside were so different that maybe he felt it and started to imagine this.

3. I realized just how much energy the narrator thought—his bones were whistling, the bullets were whizzing, the screen was shaking. It was like he got into his own little world. Later he says I took *my* girl's hand in the deepest parts. Perhaps he feels he's alone—now in his daydream or slow reaction he says the girl's his. He infers. Almost

like if he's trying to protect her. From deeper parts—that could mean maybe at looking at war from one point of view alive and energetic—he steps out, of the deeper inner reaches of himself or possibly the movie of being so involved, and actually sees what has really happened. Still life, no noise, etc. The sound track is dead could mean the people and his other state of mind maybe—the one where he feels war is great and alive.

4. I went around re-creating "Reel One" by first taking in the first things I could remember, as I went along. I already could remember some things, so I concentrated on the other verses in order to fit them into my hypothesis of the first reading—in which it's about a boy and his sense of movies with reality. Later as more sentences became clearer to me, I began to challenge my hypothesis a little to fit into the new ideas I realized I could make.

(Fifteen-year-old ninth grader)

Our Sense of Nicole's Readings

Mark: Right from her opening remarks, Nicole is attending to the voice of the speaker: "He's comparing his life to a movie."

Harold: Some readers, however, might sense that Nicole's first reading is little different from Charlene's in chapter 3. Nicole has noted the "It was like life, but better" line and imagined the movie's fantasy world as preferable to the "drab and boring" world of ordinary life, just as Charlene did.

Mark: But Charlene used primarily *her voice* to imagine her sense of the situation. Nicole's sense of the situation is based primarily on her having attended to the *speaker's voice*.

Harold: In other words, unlike Charlene, Nicole has attended to more of the author's words.

Mark: The point I'm trying to make is that Nicole is *not* attending to the words of "Reel One" as if they are the *author's words*. That's what our readers in chapters 4 and 5 were doing. They were allowing the speaking voice to be subsumed under the author's voice—as a vehicle for communicating what they thought the author was saying.

Harold: Nick says, "I think the poem was written from the point of view of an ignorant person who has been sensually dulled by television."

Mark: Nick is regarding the speaker as a *point of view,* a technique that the author uses to communicate or dramatize an idea.

Harold: As I see it, Nick is looking *at* the speaker, from outside the speaker. As a result, he judges the speaker: he's "ignorant . . . sensually dulled." In contrast, Nicole is looking *with* the speaker, from the speaker's perspective. As a result, she is able to empathize with the speaker: "The movie is his fantasy world."

Mark: Nicole is attending to the speaking voice much as we'd treat any person's speaking voice—not as primarily a mouthpiece for an implied author's ideas, but as a means to understanding another being whose particular situation is worth attending to.

Harold: And Nicole begins attending to the speaker's particular situation immediately at the beginning of her second reading.

Mark: Her statement, "Maybe he had a fight with his girlfriend," is extraordinarily different from anything we've seen!

Harold: She's trying to understand why his ordinary life outside the movies is "drab and boring."

Mark: She's trying to answer her *so what* question. Nick and Vanna were asking, Why is the *author* saying these things? What's the *author's meaning*? Nicole is asking, Why is the *speaker* saying these things? What's the *speaker's situation*?

Harold: Nicole attends to the particulars of the sensed situation as possible clues to understanding the speaker's situation.

Mark: Holding her hand in the deepest parts is "like he was searching for something that really wasn't there at all or maybe never was."

Harold: When Vanna tries to explain the hand holding, she writes, "They are ambiguous because the speaker could mean the deepest parts of the movie and the deepest parts of the snow as well."

Mark: Vanna is attending to the *author's voice.*

Harold: I don't sense that she's imagining the hand holding from the speaker's perspective when she says "deepest parts of the snow."

Mark: No, but Nicole is listening to the *speaker's voice.* She says: "He's comparing . . ."; "He describes . . ."; "It sounds like. . . ."

Harold: Nicole says that the snow with no blue "sounds like his world is totally empty and he is searching for something or someone as he looks for the non-existent blue tint to the snow." Again, she senses the speaker is searching for something.

Mark: And then she goes back to the first stanza, as if to see if she can discover what is missing from his nonmovie life. She seems to be asking: What was there about the movie experience that was so appealing?

Harold: In her first reading she had already concluded that he preferred the movies because "more is happening."

Mark: But now she seems to seek greater specificity. So when she senses that he described the movie as being about "muggings, shootings, and being in hospitals," she concludes: "He describes it as though these things don't exist in his world."

Harold: I sense, however, that she is doing much less *concluding* than *hypothesizing*. Her attempts to imagine the speaker's particular situation seem much more tentative: "Maybe he had a fight with his girlfriend"; ". . . like he was searching for something . . ."; "It sounds like his world is totally empty . . ."; "He describes it as though these things don't exist in his world." Then Nicole begins her third reading with: " 'The soundtrack was dead'—he and his girlfriend have nothing in common to share, nothing to talk about. The 'trees' could have done more talking than he did."

Mark: What an extraordinarily vivid imagining of the speaker's situation with his silent girlfriend beside him!

Harold: She seems to be asking: Why isn't he talking with his girlfriend? Why does he say there's no blue in the snow? Why does he like the movies so?

Mark: She's trying to make sense of the speaker's particular situation.

Harold: In her second reading, she proposes two hypotheses: "Maybe he had a fight with his girlfriend" and "It sounds like his world is totally empty and he is searching for something or someone. . . ." Then in her third reading, she proposes three additional hypotheses: (1) "He's a dreamer who is uninterested in reality." (2) "He is too immature or insane to handle the real world. . . ." (3) "I think he's lonely."

Mark: In her final reflections, she says, "I went about this by analyzing words with double meanings."

Harold: She imagines the possible double meanings of "I held my girl's hand, / in the deepest parts," "there wasn't much blue," "the sound track so dead," and "you could almost imagine / the trees were talking." And at the end of her third reading, she even senses a double meaning in the title, concluding that the speaker chooses the reel of the movie over the real of life. She's analyzed a lot of double meanings.

Mark: As she says, she was "Trying to picture words as they were written and thoughts behind the words. . . ." Throughout, she sustains a double focus, just as did our readers in the previous chapter. But Nicole's second focus is not on an imbedded message, but on the speaker's underlying situation. She seems to realize that, in understanding a situation, what is *unstated* is often more important than what is stated.

Harold: And I sense that she's been dealing, also, with one of her concerns: ". . . feelings of depression or loneliness that might occur in people's lives."

Our Sense of Jo Ann's Readings

Harold: I sense a lot of complexity in Jo Ann's first reading. She begins by imagining the speaker at a movie with his girlfriend, feeling ". . . great excitement like he's part of it and everything's so life-like and real." Several readers imagined the situation that way. But unlike all those readers who imagined the after-movie experience as boring, Jo Ann imagines it as almost unreal: "It's almost like too sudden a change for him, and it's so different in real life that it almost doesn't seem real. . . ." She ends being unsure about the speaker: "Maybe he feels his life isn't like that [the movies], but he wishes it were. . . ."

Mark: In attending so to the speaker's voice, Jo Ann has imagined a person who is quite unsure of what is and is not real. Her rather convoluted third sentence captures, I believe, the complexity of her imagined situation: "Maybe he's comparing the dreary snow and life to not everything that's seen on TV or movies is not always like that of real life."

Harold: I sense that her *so what* question at this point is, What exactly is the speaker's situation?

Mark: And to find the answer, she re-reads "Reel One" and gains a whole new perspective. Now she imagines a boy watching a war movie and afterward reflecting on it and on the meaning of war.

Harold: She's carefully attending to the speaker's voice and his particular choice of words in describing his film experience. Nick has also noted those words, but because he has little respect for the "ignorant person" watching the screen, he interprets those words primarily from his own perspective: "Thoughts of nurses—the perfect comforters of TV illusion. Thoughts of nice, shiny guns like nice, shiny cars. Blood so colorful and like the make-up, the gay falseness, on a dancer's face. Beautiful images of bad things. . . ." Nick, for whatever reason, has little empathy for the speaker and, therefore, doesn't try to sense the images from the speaker's perspective. Jo Ann, on the other hand, tries to imagine things from the speaker's point of view: ". . . it's almost like he's there, all in color, the guns like cars, the nurses and fighters, the dancers with their paint—almost if it's war. Soldiers against Indians. . . ."

Mark: She's attending to and is respectful of the speaker's excitement and engagement.

Harold: Then she notes the "It was like life, but better line" and reflects, "Maybe he has a love for war." She could have dismissed him as some crazy person for liking violence, as did some of our other readers. Instead, she tries to understand what the speaker is thinking and feeling.

Mark: She imagines him stepping outside on to the quiet, white landscape with the "dreary snow" and the dead soundtrack. And in that absolute silence where one can almost imagine the trees are talking, "all reality comes to him." She's seeing all of these images through the eyes of the speaker that she's imagined. And she imagines him "imagining himself in the midst of the afterpast." What a great word she's created—"afterpast."

Harold: After the excitement of the war has past, the speaker imagines and reflects on what it all might mean.

Mark: She's trying to understand what the speaker might be feeling and thinking in that state of silence after that violent movie.

Harold: She even suggests that he might be daydreaming, "trying to picture himself in the future or maybe in the past—how people in the movie would've felt."

Mark: She has such empathy for the speaker. As a result, she imagines the speaker with this incredible empathy, too, reflecting not only on himself, but on the lives of the persons who were in the movie.

Harold: How differently she imagines the speaker from Nick's interpretation of him as "sensually dulled."

Mark: But he was not attending to the voice of the speaker.

Harold: There *is* a difference. And then in her third reading, she's not content with what she's achieved. She wants even more fully to understand the speaker's situation. So she goes back to the first-stanza situation: "I realized just how much energy the narrator thought—his bones were whistling, the bullets were whizzing, the screen was shaking. It was like he got into his own little world."

Mark: Now she focuses more on the girlfriend and the line "I held my girl's hand, / in the deepest parts." In her second reading she had imagined that the speaker and his girlfriend were alone on that silent landscape. Now she's asking, What could he mean by the deepest parts? Because she's recalled his excitement with the war movie, she concludes that the deepest parts are his feelings that "war is great and alive." And she imagines the speaker wanting to protect his girl from his feelings about war, those deepest parts.

Harold: I sense that Jo Ann also imagines the speaker's wanting to exorcise those deepest parts from himself: "From deeper parts— that could mean maybe at looking at war from one point of view alive and energetic—he steps out, of the deeper inner reaches of himself or possibly the movie of being so involved, and actually sees what has really happened." And once he escapes from the clutches of his primitive nature, through this more mature ability to reflect on the aftereffects of war, the soundtrack of his love of war becomes dead. Now, some readers might say that the major problem with Jo Ann's reading is that she imagines the movie to be a war movie.

Mark: I don't think that *war movie* is the major underpinning of Jo Ann's reading. Throughout, Jo Ann's readings have been built on her imagined sense of the *emotional contrast* between the two stanzas. Jo Ann is not primarily interested in the film's genre, but in the speaker's feelings. She imagines a speaker in conflict with himself.

Harold: Her assessment of the speaker's feelings would not change if we removed the image of *war* from her readings and substituted something else. Her focus is on emotions, as her comments indicate: ". . . maybe now that the movie's gone all reality comes to him"; "It's like if he's imagining himself in the midst of the afterpast"; ". . . he sees himself in a lonely place, full of stillness . . ."; "Maybe he's daydreaming . . ."; "He's trying to picture himself in the future or maybe in the past. . . ."

Mark: The power of her reading remains. And part of the strength of her reading, in addition to her attending to the speaker's voice, is that she is continually challenging and modifying her reading as she attends more fully to that voice.

Harold: As Jo Ann says, "Later as more sentences became clearer to me, I began to challenge my hypothesis a little to fit into the new ideas I realized I could make." She keeps accommodating to the speaker's voice. Another strength of Jo Ann's reading, similar to Nicole's, is her tentativeness: "Maybe he's comparing the dreary snow and life to . . ."; "Maybe he feels his life isn't like that . . ."; "Maybe he has a love for war"; ". . . maybe now that the movie's gone all reality comes to him"; "Maybe he's daydreaming after having gone to the movies"; ". . . maybe he felt it and started to imagine this"; "Perhaps he feels he's alone . . ."; "From deeper parts . . . could mean maybe . . ."; and "The sound track is dead could mean. . . ."

Mark: All imaginings of unspecified aspects of the speaker's situation are really hypotheses.

Harold: But many readers state their hypotheses as facts. Also, I find praiseworthy Jo Ann's continual attempts to define the speaker's *emotions* in the imagined situation: ". . . he feels great excitement like he's part of it . . ."; "It's almost like too sudden a change . . ."; ". . . it almost doesn't seem real . . ."; ". . . it's almost like he's there . . ."; "It's like if he's imagining himself in the midst of the afterpast"; "It was like he got into his own little world"; and "Almost like if he's trying to protect her." Of course, you could say these are simply examples of teenage slang—"Like I'm a teenager."

Mark: Or you could say that Jo Ann is just being hesitant and vague. But I agree with you. I sense that she's trying to define as precisely as she can the speaker's feelings in her imagined sense of the situation.

Harold: So I'd argue that by inductively imagining and hypothesizing explanations for the speaker's situation and emotions, Jo Ann is able to be both specific yet open-ended in trying to make sense of this somewhat ambiguous situation.

Summary Reflections

Mark: In summary, one thing that seems pretty clear to me is that we have here two readers who are definitely asking: Who is speaking? Why would this person say these things? What is the speaker's particular situation? We haven't previously encountered this approach.

Harold: Nick thinks that the guy is sensually dulled, and Vanna thinks that he might be highly imaginative. But neither is really listening to the speaker's voice and trying to see the situation from his point of view.

Mark: And neither Nicole nor Jo Ann has any of that sense of trepidation about ruining the poem. There's a confidence in these readings that we didn't see in the readings of Nick.

Harold: Perhaps that's because Nicole and Jo Ann are much more tentative and humble in their readings. Also, perhaps it's because Nicole and Jo Ann are inductively imagining and hypothesizing possible explanations for the situation rather than trying to deal with it deductively.

Mark: They're not trying to present *the truth*.

Harold: I think we could say also that these are the first readers who have really attended to the role of the subsidiary character—the girlfriend. Previously she was just the girl whose hand was held. But in these two readings, she is more than a prop. For Jo Ann, she is someone to be protected; for Nicole, she is perhaps even a major reason for the speaker's feelings of loss and loneliness. So sensing a speaker's particular situation brings to life the other persons in that speaker's situation.

Mark: Imagining the speaker's situation enables readers to attend to the other voices in that situation, even if those voices don't actually have speaking parts. And it can't be an accident that both of these readers are female.

Harold: David was also an extremely sensitive reader.

Mark: But he was younger. The socialization process had not yet turned him into the distanced, less-empathetic male reader that research has uncovered.

Harold: Certainly the research on readers' gender illuminates what Nicole and Jo Ann are doing. For instance, David Bleich's research indicates that the women in his college classes "showed a greater willingness to construct the . . . emotional condition" of the characters and to "enter the human situations of the story more readily" than did men [1988, 149]. Yet I was reading a book recently in which the author, a male, was criticizing readers who treat characters as actual persons. To him they are to be considered as artistic creations composed of readily identified character traits that can be ticked off and posted on a chart. He believes that we should keep our critical distance.

Mark: There's a sense of power in having all these categories and structures for analyzing any text. When you identify something as a romantic poem, you know immediately what it's going to say without having to experience it. It's that old approach of treating texts as verbal objects separate from life, rather than, as Rosenblatt and others suggest, sensing them as continuous with life.

Harold: I'm trying to understand why I was so disappointed, even angry, when I read that recent book recommending that we treat characters as constructed objects and collections of character traits. Why did I find that recommendation so disturbing?

Mark: Has it got something to do with your approach to teaching being different from his?

Harold: I thought of that. As I was reading that book and sensed my displeasure with its recommended approaches—various activities and analytic systems for analyzing a text as an object—I suspected that I was upset because those recommendations run counter to the ways in which I now teach students to read. But the more I think about it, I don't sense that's an adequate explanation for my anger. I'm very able to accept and respect the fact that others teach and work with students in ways quite different from my own. That doesn't bother me. So I sense the source of my anger is deeper; it comes from some other concern.

Mark: What did reading that book remind you of?

Harold: It reminded me of the way I used to read—the way I read literature throughout most of my high school and college life. For instance, I can recall writing this enormous, structured analysis of *Anna Karenina*, a forty-three-page analysis of how Tolstoy organizes the settings of his work in order to develop his characters and themes. I wrote this in 1965 when I was working on my doctorate. And the professor wrote: "The essay is excellent. I got lost now and again in your elaborate apparatus for investigation, but your insights are rewarding throughout. A clear *A.*"

Mark: That's how you wrote most of your college papers?

Harold: Yes, during college I did a structured analysis of the types of family relationships and the patterns of imagery in Faulkner's *As I Lay Dying*. I did an analysis of how Shakespeare depicts his themes in *Antony and Cleopatra*. I analyzed the portrayal of the theme of the brother's keeper in Malcolm Lowry's *Under the Volcano*. I traced the allusions to Milton's *Paradise Lost* as I found them in Pope's "The Rape of the Lock." And now as I look back on these writings, I feel shortchanged because I don't remember anything about these works of literature. After spending a month writing my analysis of *Anna Karenina*, I can only remember that I think Anna gets run over by a train and that there was a character named Vronsky. And I can recall that I liked *As I Lay Dying* and *Under the Volcano*, but I can remember nothing else because I never made these works of literature part of my life. They were crossword puzzles that I played with. But I never stepped into the shoes of any of the characters, I never tried to sense the events from their points of view. All I did was take these methods of analysis from New Criticism, structuralism and elsewhere, and apply them. And I could do all of that and get my A's, and still never experience or be able to remember anything that I read or wrote. And that is why I feel so angry when I see a new book recommending this way of reading literature.

Mark: Did you always read this way?

Harold: No. I can recall as a child reading *The Jungle Book, Just So Stories,* and the Winnie-the-Pooh stories, and living through those experiences with the characters. I can still recall riding on the back of Bagheera, the black panther, and watching the fight to the death between Rikki-Tikki-Tavi—the mongoose—and the cobra.

Mark: It sounds as if you were experiencing the particular situations of those works. But were you sensing the particular voices?

Harold: I'm not sure. All I know is that at least I remember those stories, unlike most of the literary works that I read in college. But today, I read and write to sense the particular voices, in the manner of Nicole and Jo Ann. I don't think I'm as good at it as they are, but I'm trying. And now I not only remember what I read, but I have greater empathy for and understanding of the characters whom I would have more readily ignored or dismissed in the past.

Mark: This is the way that we've been trying to read the students and their readings in this book. Rather than categorizing them according to some analytic scheme, we've been trying to imagine and explain each reader's particular situation inductively.

Harold: I don't know how successful we've been, but I'm much happier with this approach than some analytic grid. I have a colleague who prefers the grid method of analysis so that he can then put readers' responses into a computer program and conclude that the readers from Group X use sociological perspectives to interpret the world of the text, whereas the readers from Group Y use psychological constructs. I can recall speaking to him once about my objections to that method of analysis; and when I got through speaking, he didn't respond to my ideas and situation but categorized my words according to his analytic grid. I felt as if I were nothing but an object, a dead piece of data. Yet when he puts away his analytic grid, he's a sensitive, empathetic reader of human situations.

Mark: I don't believe that we've treated our readers as objects.

Harold: But I'm not sure that we've been able to sense their particular voices, their particular situations, as fully as some of my women friends might have.

Mark: Are you implying that this is a matter of genes?

Harold: No. Although the research of Carol Gilligan [1982] and Mary Field Belinky et al. [1986] indicates that, generally speaking, men and women make sense of and deal with the world differently, they don't suggest that the difference is a matter of heredity. Males can learn to be sensitive to their own and others' feelings and to be concerned with relationships and community and continuity and mutual support. And females can learn to be competitive, to separate themselves from the concerns and needs of others, to promote hierarchical relationships, and to value analytic knowledge over empathetic understanding. Culture is a major influence.

Mark: I believe that I've become more able to attend to the individual voices of a work of literature as a result of our efforts in preparing this book.

Harold: I'm not just concerned with our being able to sense the voices of literary characters. Far more important, I believe, is the ability to understand, to empathetically understand, the particular situations of the various persons in our lives, including my own situations. As Temma Berg writes from the point of view of a feminine/feminist aesthetic, ". . . literature is deeply interconnected with life . . . we cannot separate literature from life" [1991, 187–88] and ". . . reading fosters sympathetic insight and makes us better" [192]. I want to be able to read more like Nicole and Jo Ann.

Mark: Or Tanya and Ted.

Harold: So that suggests a question, What might be the next desirable step for Nicole and Jo Ann?

Mark: Eventually to become more aware of their own voices in a situation, to situate *themselves* in the meaning-making process.

7 Tanya and Ted: Accounting for One's Own Voices of the Situation

Tanya's Readings

1. I do not especially like this poem. Since I am not looking back at the poem I can't give any specific reasons why, but I don't like the poet's choice of words—"blood as red as the paint on dancers"? What dancers? I've never seen any painted dancers—Well, O.K. maybe in that movie I saw about Amazonian Indians—O.K., so I won't trounce the poet on that. But "the trees were talking"?

Let me see how this poem relates to my own experiences—The first half of the poem seems to take place in a movie theatre—a war movie or cop movie, with lots of action and violence. Watching movies like that definitely gets your adrenalin going. The last movie like that I can recall seeing was Kubrick's *Full Metal Jacket* over the summer— And I also saw *Platoon*. For me, watching movies like that is a dual experience. In my logical, moral mind I know that war is a horrible thing, and messes up people's minds as well as their bodies, and I'd hate to be in a situation like that. But even a film like *Full Metal Jacket*, which sets out to show how abominable and dehumanizing war is, gets you excited. Violence is riveting. You imagine yourself in the character's shoes, in a dangerous, life-or-death situation. It's these situations which you don't get in day-to-day life. It's neat to imagine yourself a cold, narrow-eyed death dealer (like Clint Eastwood) or, even, in an anti-war movie which shows horrors, as suffering the martyrdom of bullets, torn and bloody, dying in glorified slow motion. When I was in my first two years of high school me and my fellow nerdish friends played *Dungeons and Dragons* every week. The game is one of imagining—you imagine yourself as a character, armed, often with magical abilities, and you troop around with your buddies and fight monsters and figure your way out of bad situations etc. There's no game board or score, so it's all in your head—it's all just talk between whoever's running the game and the players. And boy, it was great. Like a movie, it was like a real fantasy. We imagined ourselves as different personas, stronger, braver, more capable than we were in real life. There was great pleasure in imagining hacking off your enemies' heads. This allure of violence (not the *real* thing though) is what the poem seems to be expressing in its first half. It's something I feel, too, although I know better. I wonder if this is unusual for a female.

The second half of the poem stresses how dull the real world seems after the exciting movie. The snow is falling, it's monochrome, boring. I remember that after getting out of *Platoon* me and my friend had fun creeping around the subway station, pretending to elude snipers. After a movie like that, you want it to continue—you're caught up in the reality of the film. I like the poem better after reflecting on it. I think the author had a point.

2. The words in the first half contrast greatly with the second half. The first half contains exciting, vivid words, like "gleamed," "bullets," "red," "blood," "fire." The second half contains dull words like "walked," "drifts," "dead" and two "white's." Thus the difference between the vivid movie and the monotony of the outside world. There is a central irony to the poem, summed up in the line "It was like life, but better." To the narrator, the film, the fantasy, is more real than the real world. The "technicolor" film gives more stimulation to his senses than the outside world, which the author makes a winter scene, giving the reader the impression of death, lifelessness.

I sense that the narrator prefers the movie reality to the real reality. In the movie he holds his girl's hand—there's an almost sexual excitement to danger, and that line "in the deepest parts" hints he'd like to do more. The narrator seems to be an adolescent, going to the movies with his girlfriend. There is also a pun in the poem's title. "Reel One" sounds like "Real One." "Reel" refers to the actual spool of film for the movie, but the synonym "Real One" shows that irony—which version of reality is the "real" one— the exciting, sense-thrilling film, or the dull, monotonous outside?

3. The narrator prefers the exciting movie, but the author is not the narrator. The narrator seems disappointed with the winter world—the snow is boring, the trees are bare—although this scene can be quite beautiful. The author, however, has the narrator prefer some schlocky, blood-and-guts flick to it. The author has the narrator say the rather foolish line "It was like life, but better," perhaps because he's young. After all, what does the young kid know about real violence? If he

had some experience of violence, like children who've lived through war, he would not be tantalized by the movie. And yet the author is acknowledging that the fascination with violence is a real thing. The narrator is young. He's not yet learned the intellectual distaste for splatter films which adults have learned to profess, no matter what they really feel. But the author acknowledges that this fascination with violence is present in most people—it's the feeling I feel watching a violent movie, like most people. I appreciate this poem more now, but I still think the last two lines are awful.

[No fourth part was written.]

(Twenty-year-old college undergraduate)

Ted's Readings

1. "Reel One" seems to deal with two ways of seeing the world. The first way is how we see the world through movies: larger than life, loud, colorful. The second way is the way we see things from day to day, without a soundtrack to emphasize things or make them more dramatic. The way the poem is written reflects this idea. The first half is full of vivid color descriptions of blood, guns, and nurses. Reading it is almost like experiencing a movie. The second half has no color and a "dead soundtrack."

I wonder if the second half of the poem is dull only because the first half is so exciting. In other words, if the narrator hadn't gone to the film, would he see the reality in the same way? I don't think he would have. He thinks too much in terms of movies when talking about the walk home. He sees whiteness as an absence of color, not as whiteness, and quiet as an absence of a soundtrack, not as quiet. It is interesting that a movie, something that is made to imitate reality, has the property of changing our view of reality. Our narrator sees its two dimensions as being the standard to which we compare three-dimensional reality. The roles of film and reality seem to be switched. Indeed, I have to wonder which is more real to him.

2. During my second reading, one thing especially struck me which I hadn't noticed during the first reading: the presence of the girl in the poem. She is the one thing that is constantly present in the narrator's world. She is the link between whichever part of his experiences he sees as real and which he doesn't, a distinction I'm not sure of. He says that he hangs on to his girl's hand during the "deepest parts." This sounds almost as if he is afraid of falling into

the movie and losing touch with reality. During the walk home, they are silent, or at least we assume they are. Perhaps the narrator disregards anything they would have said to each other as too trivial to count after the excitement of the film and therefore doesn't even include it in his picture of reality.

During my second reading, I also looked for an explanation of the title "Reel One." I have a feeling it may refer to the question I posed before about which experience the narrator sees as reality. I don't think he is sure which experience is the fantasy and which is the "real one" or "reel one." Maybe this is stretching it, but I think this is a valuable clue when it comes to figuring out the meaning of this poem.

Before I start sounding like I'm totally against the narrator, first let me say that I share a lot of his feelings. The "real world" *does* seem dull after I come out of the movies. Even a place like Manhattan seems uninteresting after I've been bombarded with images and sounds larger than life. I suppose this is the attraction of going to the movies. Who would go to them if they weren't grander than life? This also leads to the question of whether people, if given a choice, would rather experience the world through movies than on their own.

3. With this reading, I've started to see that the narrator doesn't really make a distinction between the film and the real world as far as his role in each is concerned. He doesn't seem to include himself in either one. He is an outside observer in both.

This idea of being an outside observer could imply that the narrator is isolated from the world in the same way he is isolated from the girl he is with. He is on the outside looking in and only holds on and becomes part of it during the "deepest parts."

The narrator describes the action of the films as better than life, but their effect on him is part of his life. This is another indication that he sees himself as outside of the film as well as reality.

I don't think the real world is dull for the narrator only because it is a relatively calm night and the snowfall has colored everything white. Even if there were a fire or some other catastrophe, I don't think he would be affected by it. He might become more interested as he would in the "deepest parts" of the film, but the effect wouldn't be one of emotion or concern, merely observation.

Is Stoutenburg saying that this is happening to mankind in general? I think he is. People are becoming more and more desensitized to reality. Because the poem is written in the first person, I immediately identified it with myself and saw that a lot of things it was saying were true. Not only movies, but the structure of our society desensitizes us to the needs and feelings of other people. We are all becoming observers and actors in our world. And where there are actors without *re*-actors, the world is dull, white, and soundless, like a snowy walk home full of unfulfilled wishes.

4. The first thing I did with "Reel One" was to separate it into two parts in my mind: the part that was the movie and the walk home afterward. The division between these parts was obvious, partly because the poem physically divides itself and because the mood of the poem changes between them from frightening and violent to calm and sedate. There were bullets, guns, blood, fire, and bones. When I got to the second section, I realized that part one was being contrasted to this. Looking back, the blood was redder, the guns gleamed brighter, and the screen shook harder. I began to look at each half in relation to each other. In retrospection, I could see that these two halves represented two separate realities.

When I did my second reading of the poem, I was surprised at how differently I saw it. It no longer seemed like two distinct parts to me. I saw a bridge between these parts, something that was present in both of his worlds: the girl. Again, this violated my expectations. I saw that the worlds were connected by something and that perhaps they could be seen as parts of a whole. The illusion of two worlds was put aside, though not entirely eliminated.

With all of these ideas in mind, I looked back, in retrospect, at the title. Where I had seen no meaning before, I now saw what I can only think of as the most obvious meaning. Instead of "Reel One" I saw "Real One." This would have been impossible to see on a first reading without the question of "which half of the poem is reality?" Even now I'm seeing different ways of looking at the title. Is the narrator the "real one"? The girl? I'm no longer so positive about the meaning of the title.

I also related the text to my own experiences. When I thought about how I felt when I came out of the movies, I realized how much I feel like an observer of everything around me. Even my own words seem like part of a dialogue and don't seem to be part of me as much as they are a part of the scene around me. I put these feelings into the narrator when I stated that I saw him as an outside observer during both the film and, especially, reality.

This similarity in the way he looks at film and reality was almost a negation of the conclusion I had come to before and, quite frankly, I tried to salvage what I could of my first impressions. I concluded that while he plays an equivalent role in both the movies and in real life, that of an observer, this role changes slightly during the "deepest parts" of his observation. While I don't think this involvement would be emotional, I do think it would be a different kind of involvement. How did I come to this conclusion? I don't know. I suppose I looked at myself again and how I react to films and real-life situations. If I reacted to life the same way I react to films, as I believe our narrator does, this is the way I would feel. I think I may have changed my meaning of the poem by identifying the narrator with myself rather than myself with the narrator. I'm not sure what the difference is, but I'm pretty sure one exists and the results of each can be quite different. Perhaps I should have placed myself in the poem instead of pulling the narrator out. Keeping this in mind, I'm sure my fourth reading of the poem would bring about new ideas and shatter old ones as much as my second and third readings did. Does the process ever end?

(Twenty-year-old college undergraduate)

Our Sense of Tanya's Readings

Harold: Tanya's first words give her assessment of "Reel One": "I do not especially like this poem." Other readers might have stopped right there, but Tanya doesn't.

Mark: She turns her negative feelings into a problem and raises questions about it; that sets her off in a positive direction.

Harold: In her efforts to define the problem that she has with "Reel One," she specifies what offends her: " 'blood as red as the paint on dancers.' " Then she asks: "What dancers? I've never seen any painted dancers." And by asking that question, she gets her brain working and discovers that she *has* seen painted dancers. So she decides not to "trounce the poet." But she still raises a question about the author's final words: "But 'the trees were talking'?"

Mark: Then she reflects on how "Reel One" relates to her own experiences.

Harold: Just as Charlene did. And what are the advantages and disadvantages of doing that? Many teachers won't allow such in-depth reflecting on personal situations *during* the course of reading a work. Some teachers will promote such discussions *before* the reading begins, to prime the pump, as it were: "Class, how do you feel when you go to the movies and see an exciting film?"

Mark: Any prereading focus is going to bias the students' reading.

Harold: And rob them of doing more of the meaning making. Then there are teachers who will allow students to relate the work to their personal situations *after* the reading is completed, as David does. But how many will allow it *during* the reading, and why or why not?

Mark: Those who don't probably see it as a tangent, an interference with the main task, which they consider to be attending to the text.

Harold: But Tanya takes time out, during the course of her reading, to reflect on related situations. What does that accomplish?

Mark: First of all, we have to remember that she has read "Reel One" and has sensed clearly the general situation.

Harold: As she says, "The first half of the poem seems to take place in a movie theatre—a war movie or cop movie, with lots of action and violence." Later she says, "The second half . . . stresses how dull the real world seems after the exciting movie. The snow is falling, it's monochrome, boring."

Mark: And now her *so what* question is, as it was with Charlene, How does this "Reel One" situation relate to my own experiences?

Harold: Yet she is not doing what I think most teachers would have her do—attend only to the author's words and/or the speaker's voice.

Mark: But she *is* attending to one of the voices of the situation—*her own voice.*

Harold: And many teachers would say that if your own voice is part of the meaning making, it shouldn't be.

Mark: What we are arguing, and our data is substantiating, is that the reader's voice can't help but be a part of the sensed situation. There is no way the black marks on the page are going to come alive unless a specific reader brings them to life. And there is no way that readers can bring those words to life except by relying on their own voices—their attitudes, experiences, values, concerns. So why not allow, even encourage, students to reflect on their related situations at any point during the reading? That's what readers are doing anyway. They're continually making connections.

Harold: But I believe that it creates more focus and less clutter if teachers and students are clear about what is being emphasized at any time.

Mark: That's easy to discern in any discussion.

Harold: So, what does Tanya accomplish, in the midst of reading "Reel One," by reflecting on her own related situation?

Mark: First, it enables her to realize that "the author had a point." She begins to see some value in imagining the "Reel One" situation.

Harold: At the end of her first reading, she writes: "I like the poem better after reflecting on it." A second value of this reflecting is that it enables Tanya to learn a lot about herself. Now I can't be certain that what she reveals here is totally new to her. I suspect, however, that some of it might be. She admits that "violence is riveting," and that probably is not a new insight. But in the process of writing about the allure of violence, she reveals—and perhaps discovers—that she enjoys imagining herself not only as a "death dealer," but even as a martyr to violence. Then, after reflecting on her after-movie experience of "pretending to elude snipers," she reveals another attraction of violence—escaping it. And after reflecting on playing *Dungeons and Dragons*, Tanya articulates what might be her all-embracing motivation: "We imagined ourselves as different personas, stronger, braver, more capable than we were in real life."

Mark: She also realizes that "watching movies like that is a dual experience." Her logical mind tells her that "war is a horrible thing." Her less-logical mind finds violence "riveting." So she doesn't just have one sense of herself, but a dual sense.

Harold: A third value of taking time to reflect on related personal situations is that it prepares her to go back to the "Reel One" situation. Now that she's seen its authenticity in terms of her own life, I sense that she's ready to look more closely at "Reel One."

Mark: And to answer some of the questions that I'll wager she now has about the "Reel One" situation.

Harold: In the first paragraph of her second reading, I see her attending to the author's words: "The first half contains exciting, vivid words, like 'gleamed,' 'bullets,' 'red,' 'blood,' 'fire.' The second half contains dull words like 'walked,' 'drifts,' 'dead' and two 'white's.' "

Mark: Although she's clearly sensed the power of those words, her writing is primarily an explanation of the linguistic structure of the text. In addition, she senses and identifies "a central irony" in the "It was like life, but better" line.

Harold: Tanya concludes that paragraph still focusing on the author: ". . . the author makes a winter scene, giving the reader the impression of death, lifelessness."

Mark: But then she moves to attending to the speaker's voice.

Harold: And because she has so fully attended to her own voices and related situations, she interprets "in the deepest parts" in a way that no other reader did: "In the movie he holds his girl's hand— there's an almost sexual excitement to danger, and that line 'in the deepest parts' hints he'd like to do more." I find that a compelling imagining of the speaker's situation. And she fleshes it out by imagining the narrator "to be an adolescent, going to the movies with his girlfriend" and preferring "the exciting, sense-thrilling film" to "the dull, monotonous outside."

Mark: At the end of her second reading, Tanya senses a pun in the title, which now prompts her to turn the "like life, but better" line into a question: ". . . which version of reality is the 'real' one . . . ?" In her first reading she had identified two voices in herself—one fascinated by violence and the other decrying it. Now during her third reading, she senses two voices in the "Reel One" situation— that of the speaker and that of the implied author.

Harold: That helps produce her fabulous third reading: "The narrator prefers the exciting movie, but the author is not the narrator. The narrator seems disappointed with the winter world. . . . The author, however, has the narrator prefer some schlocky, blood-and-guts flick to it. The author has the narrator say the rather foolish line 'It was like life, but better,' perhaps because he's young. After all, what does the young kid know about real violence? If he had some experience of violence, like children who've lived through war, he would not be tantalized by the movie. And yet the author is acknowledging that the fascination with violence is a real thing. The narrator is young. He's not yet learned the intellectual distaste for splatter films. . . ."

Mark: One part of her is relating intrinsically to the experience that she imagines the speaker as having, and the other part of her is mirroring what she imagines the implied author is thinking. So we have four voices involved in her imagining of "Reel One": the two voices in herself, complexly realized, and the voices of the speaker and the implied author. Tanya's accounting for the speaking voices of the imagined situation is remarkable. But I'm bothered by her use of the word *splatter* because as complex as her reading is, I don't think either *Full Metal Jacket* or *Platoon* are "splatter films." Nor do I think they are parallel to Clint Eastwood's films. There's a kind of reduction going on. A lot of people die violently in *Platoon* and *Full Metal Jacket,* but in slow motion. The viewer is detached and can become involved in the fascination with death. There is one scene in *Full Metal Jacket* where a guy is shot to death slowly over the course of several minutes, all done in slow motion. It's horrible, but you want to rewind the video and watch it again after you've seen it.

Harold: Why?

Mark: Because—Tanya's right—there's a fascination about it. This fascination with violence, created or enhanced by the film, combines with our fascination with the total otherness, the experience of dying. The issue is raised by what she says here. At the same time, I find myself a bit disturbed finding everything lumped together as "splatter films," because I don't think that the attraction of a movie like *Friday the 13th* is really the same. But perhaps there is a connection.

Harold: My sense is that her use of "schlocky, blood-and-guts flick" and "splatter films" is a bit flip, but she's using this style throughout. She says, "O.K., so I won't trounce the poet . . . " and "There was great pleasure in imagining hacking off your enemies' heads." She's using a loose, irreverent style that enables her to be more open and revealing. One might even call her style *violent*—in that it butchers decorum and undermines expectations, yet it is appropriate for her topic. And speaking of violence, I found it fascinating that she raised a question about her reaction to violence: "I wonder if this is unusual for a female." Our data suggests that most females preferred the second stanza of "Reel One." Yet women can be fascinated by violence and can be death dealers.

Mark: What is more memorable for me, however, is the way Jo Ann imagines the "Reel One" situation. Think of the appeal of violence in movies and television and what it says about us—that we are drawn to it. Then imagine yourself in the speaker's situation as Jo Ann imagines it and ask yourself, Which is the real me? There have been times in my own life when I've reacted violently to a situation. In a sense that is a real part of who I am. Yet there's another voice in me that always argues against violence. There's a constant tension. Which is the real me? I see Jo Ann's imagined speaker experiencing that kind of tension. He knows he loves the war movie, but he's not comfortable with that part of himself.

Harold: So though you prefer Jo Ann's imagining of "Reel One" over Tanya's, your reason for doing so suggests that you're like Tanya. Personally, I don't like violent films and I try to avoid them. But I'm very attracted to Tanya's readings because of her attraction to violence and her honesty about that attraction. If I were to be more honest, maybe I'd have to admit that I've tried to hide and ignore my own potential for violence that is created when basic goals are thwarted or basic needs are unfulfilled. Perhaps I might profit from reflecting on why I avoid violent movies. So I am thankful that Tanya's readings have gotten me thinking about violence and its relationship to my own life.

Our Sense of Ted's Readings

Mark: In his first sentence, Ted says, " 'Reel One' seems to deal with two ways of seeing the world." I found that a striking way to begin.

Harold: How does Ted's reading differ from Nicole's, who said that "Reel One" was about comparing life to the movies and showing the character preferring the movies?

Mark: Ted's reading is quite different.

Harold: But isn't it similar? Ted also notes that the movies are "larger than life, loud, colorful" and that the after-movie situation "has no color and a 'dead soundtrack.' "

Mark: That's true. But Ted moves a step beyond Nicole. Nicole imagined a situation in which the character prefers movies over ordinary life. But Ted seeks to account for that preference. It's not that movies, by themselves, are exciting and that ordinary life, by itself, is boring. It's the perspective of the viewer that makes it one way or the other. And Ted is focusing on the perspective that lies behind the preferring.

Harold: But Nicole also focused on the perspective behind the preferring. The speaker may have problems with his girlfriend, and that may be why he prefers movies to ordinary life.

Mark: Perhaps I should have said that Ted's reading is different, and not a step beyond. It's a step beyond only if you value a more abstract, philosophical accounting over a more concrete, situational accounting. But that's a judgment call. Nevertheless, I see Ted's reading as different in that he's dealing with what is really an epistemological issue: ways of seeing the world. He's challenging the commonsense, positivist view that reality speaks for itself through our senses and that we play no part in perceiving what we see. As he says, ". . . we see the world through movies . . ." and " . . . we see things from day to day, without a soundtrack. . . ." Then he elaborates on this *ways of seeing the world* theme in his second paragraph: "I wonder if the second half of the poem is dull only because the first half is so exciting."

Harold: I found this reflection quite extraordinary. Most readers imagined the after-movie experience as being duller than the movie experience. But only a couple of readers sensed, as does Ted, that the speaker was using movie imagery to describe the after-movie experience: "He thinks . . . in terms of movies when talking about the walk home. He sees whiteness as an absence of color, not as whiteness, and quiet as an absence of a soundtrack, not as quiet." Only Ted noted, "It is interesting that a movie, something that is made to imitate reality, has the property of changing our view of reality."

Mark: In Ted's imagining of the situation, he does not think the narrator would have seen after-movie reality the same way if he had not gone to the movies. No other reader mentioned this.

Harold: Yet, despite the apparent clarity with which Ted seems to realize that human beings contribute to how the data before their eyes is perceived, Ted still, on occasion, sees the interpretation in the data. In his first paragraph, for instance, he says, "The first half [of the poem] is full of vivid color . . ." and "The second half has no color. . . ."

Mark: Many phrases that Ted uses indicate that he, like most of our readers, has been conditioned to talk about a text as a container of meaning. Yet so much of what he and our other readers do with "Reel One" contradicts that metaphor.

Harold: What Ted has really done is to sense a situation where the speaker is experiencing a movie "full of vivid color." As he says, "Reading it is almost like experiencing a movie."

Mark: And he hasn't sensed the situation in the way that he's made it up, but in the way that the "vivid color" is a *social construct.* If he and every other reader see "vivid color" in the first stanza, it's not because there is vivid color actually contained in that stanza, but because we all share the same social constructs—the same meanings for those words and the same values regarding those meanings.

Harold: Perhaps Ted is writing about the color that way in his first paragraph because he is focusing on the *author* by mentioning "the way the poem is written." But in his second paragraph, he switches to focusing on the *speaker's voice:* "He thinks too much in terms of movies. . . ."

Mark: Then at the end of that second paragraph of his first reading, Ted wonders which reality is more real to the speaker.

Harold: I sense that is his *so what* question, or perhaps his *next so what* question. I think that you're right when you indicate that Ted's overall theme in his readings is *ways of seeing the world.* It's not the same as Nick's thesis statement, where he has a major idea that he then seeks to support. Nor is it the same as Teresa's or Jerome's search for explanations outside of the "Reel One" situation. As I see it, Ted is using his theme as a perspective from which to explore the "Reel One" situation. I sense that Ted's overall, guiding *so what* question is something like, What are the ways in which the speaker goes about seeing the world?

Mark: In the process, he attends to other voices in the situation so that, ultimately, his *so what* question becomes, What are the ways that the speaker, the implied author, and I see the world?

Harold: Where do you hear these different voices?

Mark: There's almost a fourth voice—the voice of the girl, which he begins to explore in his second reading: "She is . . . constantly present in the narrator's world" and "She is the link between whichever part of his experiences he sees as real and which he doesn't, a distinction I'm not sure of." Ted mentions that the speaker may be holding her hand during the "deepest parts" because he may be "afraid of falling into the movie and losing touch with reality."

Harold: Charlene also saw the hand holding as enabling reality to persist for the speaker.

Mark: Yes. And during the walk home, Ted imagines the couple as either not speaking or not saying anything of significance. So, although Ted definitely senses the girlfriend at the speaker's side, he doesn't really imagine her voice in the situation. As for the speaker's voice, we've already mentioned that in Ted's first reading he senses the speaker's walk home as having been extensively influenced by the movie experience. Ted concludes his first reading by wondering which experience is more real for him.

Harold: And now in his second reading, Ted comments on the title and uses it as a "valuable clue" to decide that the speaker isn't "sure which experience is the fantasy and which is the 'real one' or 'reel one.' "

Mark: By his looking at the title as a "valuable clue," I sense that Ted is once again looking at the poem as a container with clues to the author's meaning, rather than attending to the speaker's voice.

Harold: I agree. But another way of looking at this is to say that in attending to the title, Ted is listening to the *implied author's voice.* My hypothesis is that the title often is one of the best ways to tune in the author.

Mark: That would be a more positive way of viewing what Ted is doing, though he is still, at times, locked into *container* and *clue* metaphors of meaning making as we were when we were his age.

Harold: And even when we were older. But before you go on to discuss the other ways in which Ted has attended to the speaker's voice, I think it's important to note that at the end of his second reading he takes time to attend to *his own voice:* "Before I start sounding like I'm totally against the narrator, first let me say that I share a lot of his feelings. The 'real world' *does* seem dull after I come out of the movies." So just as Tanya did, Ted stops in the middle of his reading to attend to his own voice.

Mark: I know what you mean, but you make it sound as though he puts aside his reading of "Reel One" and does something else. Attending to his own voice *is* a part of his reading of "Reel One."

Harold: I've been so conditioned to see my own voice as something separate and unrelated. Yes, Ted doesn't stop reading "Reel One." As he reads, he brings his own related situation to the foreground and moves the "Reel One" situation to the background.

Mark: In his third reading, Ted senses the speaker as viewing the world in yet another way: ". . . I've started to see that the narrator doesn't really make a distinction between the film and the real world as far as his role in each is concerned. He doesn't seem to include himself in either one. He is an outside observer in both."

Harold: And how does Ted arrive at this conclusion? First, he explains that the speaker is isolated from his girlfriend. Second, he offers a syllogistic argument that I don't fully understand. He says: "The narrator describes the action of the films as better than life, but their effect on him is part of his life. This is another indication that he sees himself as outside of the film as well as reality."

Mark: I think Ted is interpreting "better than life" as meaning "outside of or beyond life."

Harold: Therefore, if movies are outside or beyond life, and if they affect him in his real life, then both movies and reality are outside or beyond him. And that's why he is outside of them.

Mark: I guess so. But my question is, What would it mean to be inside the film or inside reality? Ted sees the speaker as detached as an observer. So to be inside would be not to be detached, but to be engaged or involved.

Harold: Probably. But the real reason I think Ted interprets the speaker as an "outside observer" is revealed in Ted's final reflections: "When I thought about how I felt when I came out of the movies, I realized how much I feel like an observer of everything around me. Even my own words seem like part of a dialogue and don't seem to be part of me as much as they are a part of the scene around me. I put these feelings into the narrator when I stated that I saw him as an outside observer during both the film and, especially, reality."

Mark: To me, that line is the most striking in all of Ted's writings about "Reel One": "I feel like an observer of everything around me."

Harold: Apparently he's done some further reflecting on his own situation, reflecting that he doesn't report here in his readings.

Mark: So Ted's imagining of "Reel One" has gone through several transformations. As he summarizes in his extraordinary final reflections, he first perceived a contrast between the two stanzas, which he saw as representing "two separate realities."

Harold: He uses again that *container* language, attributing his reading to the text "because the poem physically divides itself and because the mood of the poem changes."

Mark: But he begins by saying, "The first thing I did . . . was to separate it into two parts in my mind. . . ." And most of his final reflections reveal how fully he realizes his own active contribution to his readings. For instance, he says, "When I did my second reading of the poem, I was surprised at how differently I saw it." *He* is the one who is doing the meaning making.

Harold: In collaboration with the author's words and his own imagining of the speaker's voice.

Mark: Second, he attends to the girlfriend, sees her bridging both halves of the situation, and puts aside the "illusion of two worlds."

Harold: Third, because of how he's sensed the situation thus far, he looks back at the title and sees it in a new way. Now along with

R-e-e-l, he sees *R-e-a-l;* and he wonders which experience is the real one for the speaker.

Mark: In his final reflecting, he even revises that explanation: "Even now I'm seeing different ways of looking at the title. Is the narrator the 'real one'? The girl? I'm no longer so positive. . . ."

Harold: Fourth and finally, as a result of relating the "Reel One" situation to his own related situation, Ted concludes that the two parts of the "Reel One" situation are *not* different.

Mark: The speaker is an outside observer in both.

Harold: Now some readers might say that all Ted has done is to make the speaker more and more into an image of himself. Because, as Ted admits, he, too, feels like an outside observer much of the time.

Mark: Yes and no. Yes, Ted finally senses the speaker as an outside observer, and, yes, this is due primarily to Ted's sense of his own situation. But, no, he did not arrive at this interpretation by initially reading the text in terms of his own situation. Throughout his readings, he has continually attended to the author's words. As he says, "This similarity in the way he looks at film and reality was almost a negation of the conclusion I had come to before. . . ." Throughout his readings, he is continually allowing his expectations to be "violated." But what is even more important is that he is aware of what he is doing.

Harold: In his last paragraph he says: "I think I may have changed my meaning of the poem by identifying the narrator with myself rather than myself with the narrator. I'm not sure what the difference is, but I'm pretty sure one exists and the results of each can be quite different. Perhaps I should have placed myself in the poem instead of pulling the narrator out."

Mark: As a result of this, he realizes that "my fourth reading of the poem would bring about new ideas and shatter old ones." So he's not just creating "Reel One" in his own image. He's attending to the author's words, the speaker's voice, and, most of all, his own reading process.

Harold: Despite his occasional use of *container* and *clue* metaphors. Do you have anything else you want to say about Ted?

Mark: I just keep coming back to that line of Ted's that I quoted before, where he talks about how he feels coming out of the movies: ". . . my own words seem like part of a dialogue and don't seem to be part of me as much as they are part of the scene around me." I come back to that because a lot of the time I feel conditioned by expectations, as if I'm in somebody else's script. And no matter what I say, they're going to hear what's in their script.

Harold: I'm not so sure that's what Ted means because he doesn't give an example.

Mark: But he does! When he talks about Stoutenburg, he says: "Not only movies, but the structure of our society desensitizes us to the needs and feelings of other people." He hasn't spelled it out here, but he says, "We are all becoming observers and actors in our world." So I don't think it's just limited to the afterglow of being in a movie. It becomes a way of *being.* Now I'm not sure that's what Ted had in mind, but I think he's talking about an experience of being trapped in an observer role.

Harold: He also says, "And where there are actors without *re*-actors, the world is dull, white, and soundless, like a snowy walk home full of unfulfilled wishes." That almost brought tears to my eyes, probably because one of my deep concerns is the way so many people live lives where even their most basic wishes remain unfulfilled. To be honest, I feel that Ted speaks to me personally in this instance. As I read those lines, I sense that he is feeling that very deeply. Of course, I am sensing Ted's concerns there because I am reading those lines with my concerns there.

Mark: So having a deep concern and having that activated by one's reading is not, in itself, a problem. It might be a problem if a person is totally obsessed with one particular concern. But I sense that we all have lots of concerns.

Harold: Yes. It's not that David is concerned only about walks in the country, and that Charlene is concerned only about black holes. I believe that all of our readers have a range of concerns. And as we get older, that range of concerns broadens, I hope, so that we are more able to attend to and imagine a wide range of voices in our readings.

Mark: So what we see happening in our research is a text taking on a variety of concerns as different people bring it to life. This is really quite different from the notion that we rely only on the text and that by identifying with the implied reader, we arrive at the author's true meaning.

Summary Reflections

Mark: In summary, we can say that both Tanya and Ted are attentive not only to the words of the implied author and the voice of the speaker, but also to how their own voices and situations are contributing to their sensing of "Reel One."

Harold: Unlike most professional readers and critics, Tanya and Ted don't hide the roots of their meaning making.

Mark: And being aware of their own voices and situations, as well as accepting their contribution to the meaning making, gives them a confidence that so many of our other readers did not have.

Harold: But many of our earliest readers seemed quite confident.

Mark: Tanya and Ted's confidence is based on awareness, not on innocence. It's based on recognizing one's self as a participant in making sense of a situation. And I believe that Ted is much more aware of his own voice in the meaning making than is Tanya.

Harold: Second, I would say that being self-aware enables these two readers to know what they are and are not understanding, and what they might do next.

Mark: As I see it, making sense of a situation, both in literature and in life, grows out of the tension between different voices. And our own voices, as they are realized in the process of reading and reflecting, are as much a part of that situation as are the speaker's voice, the implied author's voice, and so on. When there's a conscious awareness of these different voices, readers have the means for revising and enriching their readings over time.

Harold: And both these readers, especially Ted, seem to be aware that imagining the situation is an unending process. As Ted comments, "Does the process ever end?"

Mark: They realize that there's always another question that can be asked, another perspective that can be taken, another insight that can be gained through another reading.

Harold: What might be the next desirable step for each of these readers?

Mark: As you said, they are already aware of their next steps. Tanya can't stand the last lines of "Reel One": "You could almost imagine / the trees were talking." If she is to deepen her understanding of the speaker, she needs to attend to those lines and be more aware of her own role in disliking those lines.

Harold: And Ted is aware that he may have identified the speaker with himself rather than himself with the speaker. I think he's right. Because Ted sees the world from the perspective of an observer and has imagined the speaker that way, Ted has had difficulty imagining what "the deepest parts" might be. He says, ". . . I don't think this involvement would be emotional, . . ." but he's not yet been able to clarify this part of the situation.

Mark: I think that's his next step.

Harold: The questions that I still have, however, are these: To what extent are readers able to broaden their own perspectives, to move beyond their own voices? Can Marxists or Freudians or feminists ever read in ways that are different from their chosen perspective?

Mark: Insofar as their perspective is chosen, insofar as they are aware of having chosen it, of course they can read from a different perspective. But usually they don't choose to. As for younger readers who have not yet acquired a range of culturally defined perspectives, they also can choose from among their multiple concerns and memories of related situations—providing that they also are aware of their role in the meaning-making process.

Harold: A related way of expanding one's own perspective is to be aware of other people's ways of seeing the world. This has certainly been my experience in reading these readings with you.

Mark: Likewise.

III Empowering Students' Readings of Literature

8 What Disempowers Meaning Making?

There are many school-based practices that disempower readers' abilities to make meaning: assigning books and book reports as the major way to promote a love of reading; providing background information, lists of vocabulary words, purposes for reading, and follow-up questions as the major way to enable students to read texts; and using tests and theme papers as the major way to evaluate students' reading abilities. Usually students have little power to counter these disempowering practices—except to label them as *school reading* and to dissociate such activities from *real reading*. But what *reader-based* practices are disempowering?

Being Unable to Sense the Situation

Approximately one-third of our eleven to twelve year olds were unable to sense the general situation of "Reel One" after three attempts. We hypothesize that these beginning readers used at least five different approaches in trying to make sense of "Reel One." Let us see how effective each of these ways of reading is.

The first approach was *expressing a general statement* about the reading. One of these readers, for instance, is able to express only a general evaluation: "I think that it is an interesting poem though I don't understand it much." Another reader is able to express only a general feeling: "It gave me an odd feeling." Certainly it is better to say something than nothing, but a reader needs to be able to do more.

The second approach that some of these beginning meaning makers used was *attending only to isolated words.* Here, for instance, is eleven-year-old Quincy's readings:

1. war   hospitals   winter   red oak trees

2. ballet   painters   blood   my hand

3. rainbows   whistles   tires   snow

4. I read it little by little and every time I noticed new ideas. I don't understand what it's about, but I saw mixed ideas in there.

For the most part, Quincy is either recalling words verbatim (e.g., "trees," "blood," "my hand") or giving related associations (e.g., "winter" for "snow," "ballet" for "dancers," "tires" for "track"). This is a step beyond just seeing the text as a blur and being able to express only a general statement about it. But, obviously, a reader needs to attend to more than isolated words.

The third, fourth, and fifth ways of beginning meaning making are illustrated by twelve-year-old Irene's readings. Her first reading attempts to sense the general situation of "Reel One":

> 1. I think that this poem sounds like a war hospital, with the blood and nurses.

Certainly *sensing a rudimentary situation* is a step beyond looking at isolated words and brainstorming related associations. Irene's second reading senses a contrast within the situation:

> 2. I noticed that the first setting was violent and bloody, and in the second setting the poet talked about snow, and holding hands, and more peaceful and relaxed things.

Sensing contrasts is one of our major ways of making meaning, as Robert Scholes indicates: "The first things to look for [in reading] are repetitions and oppositions that emerge" (1985, 32). But Irene seems unaware that this approach could help her, as indicated in her last reading:

> 3. I noticed that the poet uses similes to emphasize his point. "The guns gleamed like cars." I also noticed that the poet uses personification in the last line—"the trees were talking."

Identifying figures of speech, however, does not enable Irene to interpret them and make sense of "Reel One."

Irene may be resorting to identifying figures of speech in her last effort to make meaning because it is so often how readers are taught to interpret texts. The assumption is that one cannot possibly make sense of a work without knowing a special vocabulary and identifying the work's rhetorical elements. And what happens when readers use this approach to make meaning?

Here are what three eleven-year-old males did with this approach: (1) "The poet uses many comparisons"; (2) "I like all the similes and metaphors the author gives"; and (3) "The first paragraph reminds me of when I was in elementary school last year when we were learning similes and metaphors." And what were the results? *None of the readers who labeled figures of speech were able to interpret those elements, and almost all of the readers who interpreted successfully the "Reel One" figures of speech did so without labeling them.*

Although it is easy to identify examples of simile and personification, such an ability does not enable readers to interpret these figures of speech. And being able to sense whether something is ironic, or metaphoric, or hyperbolic, or symbolic is even more difficult. Wayne Booth helps us understand this situation when he tells this anecdote in *A Rhetoric of Irony:*

> I once had a student who wrote a paper about the joys of deer hunting, including a vivid description of the thrill that "coursed through" his veins as he cut the deer's throat and watched the life dying in those "large, beautiful, child-like eyes." It was evident to me that he was satirizing blood sport. But I found, in what seems now to have been one of the most ineffectual conferences I have ever had with a student, that my ironic reading was to him plain crazy. I made the mistake of lingering over his bloodthirsty phrases, trying to explain to him why I had thought them ironic. But he was simply baffled, as well he might be; to read irony in any one of his statements was to misunderstand his entire perception of what his life and the deer's were all about. Wrestling with irony, he and I were not talking only about "verbal" matters; we were driven into debate about how a man should live. (1974, 38)

Why did Booth, a master reader and the author of a book on irony, have such difficulty sensing whether the students' ideas about deer hunting were to be taken literally or figuratively? Because something is nonliteral only when it does not seem to accord with our usual way of sensing the world, and because Booth's way of sensing the world of deer hunting and his student's way were totally different. We recall what one of our readers of "Reel One" remarked: "I don't find anything ambiguous in this poem. It is all straightforward and clearly written." Most figures of speech, therefore, cannot be identified in isolation and certainly cannot be adequately interpreted without a sense of the situation. Knowing the definitions of various figures of speech will not help. That is why the reader who says, "That sounds funny! What does the author mean by that?" is much further ahead than the reader who says, "There's a simile." After all, people have been using and interpreting figures of speech long before they were labeled.

Does this mean that we should not help students develop a

vocabulary for identifying rhetorical elements? Suppose a student reads the phrase "Less is more" and then comments, "How can that be? That's a contradiction!" Should we at that point label the figure of speech that she is trying to figure out? We believe that we would be more helpful by asking, "Can you think of a situation in which something that seemed less was actually more?" And then when she gives some examples of that paradox and says, "Hey, that's neat. What is that called when you say something that seems a contradiction but really isn't?" we can mention the technical term. We believe that we can more fully empower readers by attending to their meaning-making situations than by drilling them on the definitions of literary terms.

Then what reading approaches did enable some of our beginning meaning makers to sense the situation of "Reel One"? *Sensing contrasts* helped Irene, but by itself it was not enough. What helped more was *inductively imagining and explaining the situation.* Twelve-year-old Sam uses this approach:

> 1. I didn't understand that poem very much, but it seemed like the two people are survivors from a nuclear war and walking around observing the ruins.
>
> 2. Now it seems like the poem takes place in the winter in the woods after a hunt, and a father and daughter leave what is left of the hunting grounds.
>
> 3. Now it seems like the poem is describing a cowboys and Indian shootout in a movie theater. The two people leave and walk home.
>
> 4. Everytime I read the poem I imagined a different thing. I think my descriptions of the poem get better every time.
>
> When I wrote what I did, I only really wrote down what came to my mind first and what seemed obvious at that time.

Sam pays attention to enough details to be able to form hypotheses, yet he does not overelaborate each of his depictions of the "Reel One" situation. Thus he is able to revise his hypotheses—so that they "get better." Sam is, we believe, a most competent reader. But even though he finally is able to sense the general situation of "Reel One," how meaningful a reading experience has this been for Sam?

And how meaningful a reading experience was it for the 75 percent of our eleven and twelve year olds who were either unable to sense the general situation of "Reel One," or able to sense the general situation only after three readings? The best way to find out, of course, is to ask the students. But in lieu of being able to do that, we hypothesize: If readers are unable—on their own—to sense the outline of the general situation, the text is too difficult.

Being Critical or Being Immersed

While we believe it is important that readers feel empowered enough to stand up for their own values and criticize what they dislike, we sense that such an approach—by itself—will not enable them to understand another's situation. A more powerful stance would be to try to be respectful of another's situation and save the criticism until afterward. But sometimes this is impossible. Sometimes it is necessary for readers to take a detour before they can get on the highway. And sometimes that detour is the highway.

One of our graduate student readers, Yvette, was incensed by her sense of the "Reel One" speaker:

> I don't like this poem. I don't like the kind of person who likes this kind of movie. I don't like this person because he said it was better than life. He probably ate a large bucket of popcorn and dug at the bottom of the box with his fingers. I hate people who do that. He probably had a large coke, then chewed the ice after the liquid ran dry. When he held his girl's hand, his hand was probably greasy and salty. People who enjoy that kind of movie don't know enough to wipe off their hands. People who date guys like that have incredible tolerance for ice chewing and popcorn noises. They make very good wives. She probably didn't notice a thing.
>
> What "deepest part"? The deep part of her lap? Such movies don't have deep parts unless you have a Rambo I.Q.

In the process of expressing her dislikes, Yvette is able both to imagine vividly a movie-going situation and to attend to some of the text. Although we may have wished that Yvette had been more attentive to the second stanza of "Reel One" and been less judgmental of "Rambo I.Q." persons, we realize that there are limits to what most of us are able to tolerate. So, what might be a next appropriate step for Yvette? If she had shared these initial readings of "Reel One" with a small group of her trusted classmates (rather than with her teacher or the entire class), then we hypothesize that she would have been able to broaden those first impressions upon hearing how other readers sensed the situation and speaker of "Reel One." In addition, since Yvette was planning to be a teacher, she might have found it helpful to reflect on the students whom she would be willing to teach.

Another reader, eighteen-year-old Brad, was also incensed by his sense of the values expressed in "Reel One":

> The first group of lines shows how everything can be made to be perfect. Like everybody says, "It's just like in the movies."
>
> Well, that's a crock. In the movies everything turns out just the way you want it to, provided you have enough money to finance your stupid dream. In real life, no matter how hard you try, you get screwed in the end. Even if you have all the money in the world, you really don't have anything.

As with Yvette, reading "Reel One" has engaged one of Brad's present concerns: the impossibility of people realizing their dreams. Brad, however, writes so extensively about his concerns (three times as much as we have quoted) and so little about "Reel One," that we hypothesize he would profit most from writing specifically, extensively, and reflexively about his own concerns—the real highway for him at this time.

Unlike Yvette and Brad, eleven-year-old Harriet was critical of the *form* of "Reel One":

> It sounded like haiku to me, and I hate haiku because it feels too limited. I think that a poem should be something that just flows and you can say what you want and how you feel. Something else that I didn't like was the scene changing from the movies to outside and the snow. Because I think poems should stay on one feeling like anger or fear or love or caring.

If Harriet could be helped to realize that there is a contradiction in her evaluative criteria, and if she could be persuaded to experience the "Reel One" situation rather than criticize it, then perhaps she would not have concluded her writing by saying, "Why the hell he called it 'Reel One' I don't think I'll ever know."

Dealing with critical readers can be unnerving, especially when they find objections to works that we treasure, or respond in ways that we cannot immediately appreciate and understand. But we hypothesize that critical readers may be some of our most intelligent and sensitive readers. If we can enable these readers to transform their criticisms into specific questions and then help them find ways to explore answers to those questions, we believe that we all will profit.

After all, Tanya (chapter 7) began her reading of "Reel One" with a criticism: "I do not especially like this poem." But by turning that criticism into a question ("What dancers? I've never seen any painted dancers"), Tanya was able to overcome her objection ("Well, O.K. maybe in that movie I saw about Amazonian Indians") and continue her exploration.

The vast majority of our readers, however, were not critical of any aspects of "Reel One." When twelve-year-old Bonnie recalls the phrase "It was like life, but better," for instance, she writes:

> How could she feel that blood and terror are better than life itself the way life goes? She has her own thoughts, but I feel that life should be a pleasure with hard times and work but not all terror and bone chills.

Bonnie concludes her third reading by writing:

> And at the end when it started to be peaceful, she said it was dead! How could a pretty winter night be dead? But I have my own ideas. I love cold winter nights.

The first step in dealing with points of view that seem different from our own is to grant other persons the right to their different opinions. A more difficult step, of course, is to try to understand those different perspectives. Bonnie takes the first step—by respecting and not rejecting or criticizing what is different from her own way of seeing the world.

In contrast to readers who are being critical, we have readers who are *being immersed,* by which we mean *imagining a work so myopically that one is unable to distinguish between one's own situation and the situation of another.* In all of our 288 sets of readings, however, we could find no reader who was completely immersed. One reader who came close to being immersed was a twenty-two-year-old graduate student, Daphne, who wrote:

> I was able to pick up that the poem was describing some kind of war movie. . . . A couple had gone to see the movie. . . .
> Somehow (I must confess to probably having seen too many *M*A*S*H** reruns) I was picturing or hearing the accompanying soundtrack of a *M*A*S*H** episode, during an attack scene. There are people running in every direction. Some were carrying others, and some were dripping with blood which contrasted with the drab green scene I am imagining (which seems odd because

when I think back I can't at this point recall the color green or khaki being mentioned). . . .

The idea of snow falling in this scene (this isn't part of the movie anymore though) doesn't work for me. . . . The idea of "white and more white" works well, but it may be more effective here to use gray. White though is how I picture their skin tone from the shock. . . .

I still see only drab greens and smoke and the guns hardly shine with all the dust flying about. . . .

Stoutenburg took otherwise meaningless events and gave enough inference to create a scene in the reader's (my) mind. . . . The poem itself created all its own images and perceptions for me.

Throughout her reading, Daphne seems to be somewhat aware of the differences between her own sense of the situation and the author's. Yet at no point in her writing does she revise her imaginings to accommodate the details of the text. Even more surprisingly, this graduate student and English major seems totally unaware of her own role in the meaning-making process; for in her final reflections, she comments twice on how the author and the poem made her read the work the way she did. If Daphne is to be a better reader, we believe that she needs to be less immersed.

Being critical and *being immersed* may seem to be opposites, but we hypothesize that they are two sides of the same coin. Persons who read this way are confusing and conflating their own concerns and situations with the concerns and situations of others. The solution is not for these readers to suppress their own voices, but to distinguish between their own voices and the voices of others.

Abstracting a Theme Statement

When we read certain texts—fables, parables, allegories, satires, science fiction, many fantasies—we often sense that they were written, at least in part, to communicate one or more major ideas. And many of us may be inclined to read these texts and others, at least in part, for the purpose of figuring out and abstracting their underlying or over-riding idea. In fact, the ability to go from the concrete to the abstract is often regarded as one of the major goals of cognitive development. It is natural, therefore, for some readers, at the end of their reading, to try to summarize their sense of a work with a theme statement.

But there are two questions that we would like to raise about the practice of reading for the purpose of abstracting a theme statement: What happens when persons read a text *primarily* for the purpose of abstracting a theme statement? What is gained by trying to wrap up or close down one's reading of a work of literature by reducing it to a theme statement?

Let us begin with the first question. Initially we found that only 1 percent of our original 270 readers (three students) sought primarily to abstract a theme statement from "Reel One." Realizing that our instructions had invited students to *re-create* "Reel One," we sought to find out what would happen if we changed the instructions. So we went to an extra group of eighteen students (high school seniors) and asked them: "Write an analysis of 'Reel One.' Explain what you think this poem means and how it conveys this meaning to you." In contrast to our earlier findings, 17 percent of these new readers (three out of eighteen) sought immediately and primarily to abstract a theme statement from "Reel One." Despite our invitation to do otherwise, however, 83 percent of these readers (the other fifteen) focused on making sense of the particular situation or the speaker of "Reel One." But what happens when readers seek initially and primarily to abstract from a text a theme statement?

The first of two major approaches that our readers used was *abstracting a theme statement based on sensing a contrast within the general situation.* Seventeen-year-old Vincent senses that "Reel One" is about "both violence and peace," indicating that the first-part "description of a drama film" has "images of guns, bullets, blood and fire," whereas the "second part has a description of a couple walking home on a beautiful evening." Then, instead of enhancing his beginning sense of this general situation, Vincent abstracts a theme statement:

> Life in the city would be very different from life in the country. The city life seems to be moving at a quicker pace. The country would be less active and more beautiful. The country represents how life should really be.

The second of two major approaches that our readers used was *abstracting a theme statement based on interpreting isolated elements.* We have already looked at our one example of this method: Teresa's readings (chapter 3). As we saw, Teresa makes little effort to explore her initial summary of the "Reel One" situation; and when she encounters the evaluative phrase "It was like life, but better," she does *not* try to integrate it into her sense of the moviegoing situation.

Instead, she treats the phrase as a logical proposition and uses syllogistic reasoning to interpret it: If "It" refers to "guns" and "blood," which signify "death," and if "death is like life but better," then this is "a poem about Death leading to a new and better life." In essence, Teresa's theme statement regarding "Reel One" is *Death is better than life because it leads to a new and better life.*

A slightly different version of this second approach is eighteen-year-old Anna-Marie's way of reading "Reel One." Unlike Teresa, who begins her reading with a sense of the general situation of "Reel One," Anna-Marie begins immediately to abstract a theme statement by noting only the first elements of the text: "'Reel One' seems to be talking about the insignificance of some happenings." She then supports her thesis by describing the first isolated elements:

> It sounds like there was a gunshot, but it sounded very strange. The poem says the guns "gleamed," making them sound enticing and nice to look at. The blood was a pretty color and is compared to the red face of a dancer. That sounds like a *good* image—but blood from a gunshot wound is not a nice thing. This may represent the insignificance of the gunshot.

Then when she senses the snow imagery—"too much snow, too much white"—she uses this isolated element as further support for her thesis: "I think this snow image represents our ability to hide things. *We* make things seem insignificant." By the end of her reading, Anna-Marie has identified elements to support her theme statement, but like many of our eleven and twelve year olds, she has little sense of the general situation of "Reel One."

Another variation of this second approach is the reader who does not try to herd all elements under the roof of one abstraction, but who allows each isolated element to suggest a different thesis. Thus seventeen-year-old Sally, as she peripatetically reads "Reel One," offers the following attempts to abstract theme statements: (1)"The poem's meaning to me is how complex life is and how we depict it through movie reels"; (2) "But then he goes on to show the tranquility of life and how there has to be a balance of chaos and total tranquility"; (3) "The second part shows how tranquility and peacefulness can be shared with another person"; (4) "Then he shows how you can really personify non-living things and make them full of action like a gun or car"; and (5) "He also shows the connection two people can have without words." We can see how easily this approach could be used to develop themes from any series of actions: going to the grocery store shows that people need to eat; opening the door shows that our hands can help us; using a grocery cart shows that humans have invented useful tools; selecting our groceries shows we have freedom of choice. . . .

Now none of these students is a poor reader; in fact, we sense that each is quite clever. And if the primary goal is to abstract a theme statement almost immediately from the text, they all have succeeded. The question we ask, though, is, What are they gaining by doing this? Or as literary scholar Wolfgang Iser asks: ". . . what can be the function of interpretation if its sole achievement is to extract the meaning and leave behind an empty shell?" (1976, 5).

Unlike Vincent, Teresa, Anna-Marie, and Sally—who immediately seek to abstract a theme statement based on only a cursory sense of the *general* situation—some readers allow themselves time to sense the *particular* situation before trying to abstract a theme statement. Nick and Vanna do this successfully in chapter 5. But some readers are less successful in their attempts. Here, for example, is how twenty-year-old Rosita, an English major, deals with some particulars of the "Reel One" situation in an effort to abstract a theme statement:

> The poet says there was no blue outside, just white snow everywhere. White symbolizes good which suggests that the world is full of goodness. Yet this white is artificial; it covers up all the distress and the evil, preventing anything blue/real to appear. . . . It expresses a pessimistic view of life as the poet suggests that there is only hypocrisy in this world which covers up reality.

In an effort to dig out a big, hidden meaning, Rosita isolates images from the situation in which she first sensed them, using her personal dictionary of stock symbols to interpret "white" as symbolizing "good," and "blue" as symbolizing "distress" and "evil." Then she becomes immersed in her evoked concerns, claiming that "the poem suggests that there is only hypocrisy in this world which covers up reality." In her attempts to uncover a theme statement, Rosita loses her sense of the situation of "Reel One" and reiterates a concept about hypocrisy that she had repeated in several of her other interpretations throughout the semester.

Now let us look at our second question: What is gained by trying to wrap up one's reading of a work of literature by reducing it to a theme statement? Nick (chapter 5) tries to summarize the essence of "Reel One" when he states that it "was written from the point of view of an ignorant person who has been sensually dulled by television and its bigger-than-life panorama." Yet Nick is aware, as we noted in chapter 5, that he "disregarded certain lines" in order to produce this "punchline"; and he realizes that it is "ridiculous" to assume that he has understood "the 'meaning' of the poem." Unlike Nick, Vanna (chapter 5) is less concerned with trying to condense "Reel One" into a theme statement. So she ends her readings with a question: ". . . just which 'reel' are we playing here anyway? The reel of a movie or the reel of the speaker's imagination?" Whereas Nick tries to close down his sense of the "Reel One" situation by concluding that TV has dulled the speaker, Vanna's leaves open her sense of the meaning of "Reel One."

Two other readers who sensed and were able to keep in focus the *particular* situation of "Reel One," as they sought to abstract a main idea from it, came up with these theme statements: "Movies are 'better' because they wake up that imagination that takes the reality of the Planet Earth for granted" and "Art does not evoke the imagination and deeper levels of consciousness. Life does." What we find ironic about these two theme statements is that they contradict each other. Now certainly it is natural for readers to try to deal with the complexity of a work of literature by summarizing it in terms of a theme statement. But what have they really gained by doing this? And what have they lost?

This leads us to a third question that we would now like to consider: How might we talk about *themes* in a more helpful way? One way of exploring possible answers to this question is to look at what professional readers do when they write about literature. As a result of reading numerous reviews of works of literature, we hypothesize that professional readers do not usually reduce works to theme *statements*. Usually they use the term *theme* to identify the work's *situational focus* or *thematic concern*.

In a drama review of a production of *Of Mice and Men*, for instance, Mel Gussow writes of "the play's theme of loneliness" (1987, C24). And when Max Alexander writes about the fiftieth-anniversary restoration of *Gone with the Wind*, he says, "If the novel has a theme, the theme is that of survival" (1987, H13). *Loneliness* and *survival* are not theme *statements*; they specify what the reader senses is the work's situational focus or thematic concern. Furthermore, we sense that each descriptor is based on the critic's sense of the *particular* situation, making the designation of theme specific and yet general enough to enable the critic to explore all aspects of the work within the specified theme's circumference. Similarly, when Northrop Frye writes, "In *Huckleberry Finn,* the main theme is . . . the freeing of a slave" (1957, 180), he is not giving us a theme statement, but a phrase that identifies one aspect of the work's situation and that indicates there are others. And in a book review of Mary Gordon's *The Other Side,* when Michiko Kakutani lists what she senses to be the themes of Gordon's earlier novels, she does not present these themes as statements: "The limitations and failures of love, the hazards of ordinary life, the dangers of self-sacrifice and the difficulties of reconciling an ideal (in this case, the ideal of family responsibility) with the contingencies of daily existence—these themes, raised by Ms. Gordon's earlier novels . . ." (1989, C21). For Kakutani, themes are particular human situations that Mary Gordon has explored. How fatuous it would have been to present them as statements: "Mary Gordon says that love is limited and can fail, that ordinary life is hazardous, that there are dangers in self-sacrifice . . ."!

The most helpful way that we have found for talking about themes is to speak of them as *thematic questions.* As we see it, many writers begin not with a thesis or proposition to be expressed but with a situation to be explored; and one way of exploring that situation is by sensing it and then asking questions about it. Thus instead of talking to our students about *theme statements* or *themes,* we speak about the work's *thematic concerns and questions.* Others also regard themes as concerns and questions. When John Caird (1987) talked about his directing of *Les Misérables,* for instance, he said: "One of the main themes of the novel and the musical is, 'What is man's relationship to authority, to order?'" And when Denis Donoghue discussed Robert Merton's *On the Shoulder of Giants,* he wrote: "True, it has a good theme—what constitutes knowledge, how is it discovered, and in what bizarre forms is it transmitted?" (1985, 34).

When readers sense a situation's thematic concerns and questions, those readers are able to explore that situation rather than stuffing it into a statement. Had all of our readers regarded *theme* as concerns and questions to be explored, rather than as theses to be abstracted, we would not have had students condensing "Reel One" into these statements: "The country represents how life should really be"; "Death is not an end; it is rather, a new beginning"; "*We* make things seem insignificant"; "there is hypocrisy in this world which covers up reality"; "Movies are 'better' because they wake up that imagination that takes the reality of the Planet Earth for granted"; "Art does not evoke the imagination and deeper levels of consciousness.

Life does." Imagine, therefore, student readers sensing and exploring the thematic concerns of "Reel One," at various stages of their reading development, by asking: What is the experience of going to the movies? How are movie life and nonmovie life related? What is real and how do we respond to it?

Summary

Throughout this chapter we have explored one thematic question: What disempowers meaning making? And by inductively imagining and explaining the situations of several disempowered readers, we have discovered the same problem. Whenever readers try to make sense of something—be it to ascertain what is happening, or what a particular word or phrase means, or what a text might signify—such meaning making falters when readers ignore or fail to attend to a sense of the situation. Words, events, perceived figures of speech, or thematic concerns can be adequately understood only when readers are able and willing to sense the situation—of both themselves and others. Note, once again, the difference between the unsituated and the situated reader:

> I think it is a fairly lousy poem. I'm not getting many connections with it, to it from without. It's just sitting there. It seems disjointed. "My bones whistled"—this, now that I look at it, is probably the most apt line to describe the speaker. Bones that whistle are hollow, so he must be hollow, shallow.
>
> (Celeste, twenty-two-year-old college undergraduate)

> Yeah, he's definitely watching an action movie with his girlfriend. Everything is happening all at once, but it's beautiful, just like the movies, not dull as real life, and his little body is screaming with excitement, his bones are whistling.
>
> (Ken, twenty-two-year-old college undergraduate)

9 What Empowers Meaning Making?

Obviously there are many factors that *support* meaning making: having sufficient physical health, mental ability, and sensory acuity to be able to attend to a text; sharing enough of the requisite language and culture for at least some communication to occur; and having a beginning familiarity with texts and how to use them. But what *empowers* readers to give a text life and value?

Sensing and Making Sense of the Situation

Overall, from looking at 288 student readings of Adrien Stoutenburg's "Reel One," we sense that successful readers are *situated readers* who begin by asking questions such as: What's going on here? Who's doing what, how, to what effect, and why? Who is speaking? What does this remind me of? Do I care? Who am I as I try to answer these questions? Once these readers have sensed an outline of the situation, then they strive to enhance their understanding of that sensed situation. And how do they do that? Let us explore two pairs of concepts that we have found useful in characterizing how readers make sense of situations: being deductive, being inductive; explaining, imagining.

Deductively Explaining. One of the easiest ways of making meaning is by *deductively explaining* the situation. *Being deductive* means that the meaning maker begins with a hypothesis and attends to only those details that support it. By *explaining*, we refer to the act of *stating, analyzing, defining, categorizing, and arguing one's sense of a situation.* Nick (chapter 5) vividly demonstrates how he makes meaning by deductively explaining the poem. As he strives to prove that "the poem was written from the point of view of an ignorant person who has been sensually dulled by television," he admits: "I disregarded certain lines because I wasn't sure if they fit my idea." Albert (chapter 2) also is deductively explaining as he strives to refine his initial summary of "Reel One": "I thought it was a guy and a girl going to the movies together and then home." And Teresa (chapter 3) deductively explains—through the manipulations of syllogistic logic—how "It was like life, but better" can mean "Death is not an end; it is rather, a new beginning." Overall, we sense that readers who chose to explain their sense of the "Reel One" situation deductively were the least able to revise and thus enhance their first impressions of that situation.

Inductively Explaining. An approach that more adequately allows readers to make sense of a situation is *inductively explaining.* As with all meaning making, both deductive and inductive thinkers begin with a sense of the situation, some overall hypothesis of what is happening. In contrast to deductive thinkers, however, inductive thinkers regard their initial sense of the situation as tentative and open to revision as new and unanticipated aspects arise. Our two examples of readers who inductively explain the "Reel One" situation are Jerome and Ted. Jerome (chapter 4) revises his explanation of the situation three times by shuffling around various elements of "Reel One" from one context to another in an effort to interpret them. Ted (chapter 7) also revises several times his sense of the "Reel One" situation and his interpretations of the details within it. And at the end of his extensive explorations, Ted asks, "Does the process ever end?" While we question some of Jerome's assumptions about reading (e.g., he envisions that as a teacher his job will be "to bring out as many interpretations as possible"), nevertheless, we sense that both Jerome's and Ted's way of *inductively* explaining the situation empowered them more fully to explore "Reel One" than did Albert's, Teresa's, and Nick's way of *deductively* explaining it.

When we say that readers are *explaining*—whether deductively or inductively—we do not mean that they are not also *imagining.* In one sense, it is impossible to think without imagining. As cognitive psychologist David Taylor explains: "The visual images that are formed and re-formed, the words that are 'heard' in the mind when we talk to ourselves, the 'sounds' of notes and chords or the 'feelings' of various signs and movements— all these are made possible by the faculty of imagination, the ability to re-create perceptual experiences on demand" (1983, 72–73). Thus, when we interpret someone's reading as *explaining their sense of the situation*, we realize that the reader had to engage in imagining in order to be able to explain; but we sense that explaining—not imagining—was at the forefront of that meaning making.

Deductively Imagining. In contrast with explaining, *imagining* provides us with an even more powerful way of reading. By *imagining* we do not mean being *fanciful* or *imaginary*; instead, we refer to the act of *visualizing, hearing, feeling, synthesizing, and portraying one's sense of a situation.* Our two examples of readers who are *deductively* *imagining* "Reel One" are David (chapter 2) and Patrick (chapter 4). Each of these readers begins with a summarized sense of the general situation and then proceeds through subsequent readings to expand that summary by imagining the general situation in greater detail. Thus David goes from "walking in the snow" to "walking down Bullet Road to home so many miles away with a girl at his side and her hand in his. The countryside was silent. There was not a whisper to be heard. The snow was falling and it was night." And Patrick moves from "A guy watching a horror film with his girlfriend" to "A guy watching a movie, horror, maybe 3-D. Colors seem amplified, guns shine brightly, and blood is redder. Explosion on the screen, he shivers in tension and fright." We sense that Patrick is doing a bit more explaining than is David, especially when Patrick interprets the title; but overall we hypothesize that he is primarily *imagining*. Furthermore, we hypothesize that being able and willing to imagine a situation, in rich detail, is an unmistakable feature of engaged, empowered reading.

Inductively Imagining. Several of our younger readers— those who initially were unable to sense the general situation— engaged in the process of *inductively imagining*. Sam (chapter 8), for example, inductively goes through two *summarized* imaginings of "Reel One" before concluding: "Now it seems like the poem is describing a cowboys and Indian shootout in a movie theater. The two people leave and walk home." In contrast, Kim inductively develops her sense of "Reel One" by imagining it *in detail* in her readings:

> 1. It's very lively and animated at first. Not quite clear, but animated. The new paragraph begins and all turns cold and colorless. I imagine white snow all over, but the trees are still green, though all else is a dull grey or white.
>
> When animated, it's like a colored, old-fashioned (50s) cartoon. With a bright red car from the 50s. Not quite clear what kind, but it's bright red with silver chrome bumpers, and all that's not red (besides the black tires) is silver. I see a screen with red blood shooting through it.
>
> Those were my first impressions.
>
> 2. Not many different interpretations this time. More color though. Now, instead of blood spurting through the screen, I see it on fire with flames. It reminds me of a photography darkroom. Don't know why, but it does. Like before, I sense all of these "technicolor" objects more or less on a comic page. And in dead center, there's a huge pistol, gleaming with silver.

The car is set in black, kind of slanted—can't explain. Only the gun, car, and burning (bloody) screen are visible. There's a nice blue background, like sky. All else is not clear.

3. Now I see a drive-in movie. There was a shoot out and blood all over. Bullets from the gun shoot out. I see two dancers with red splashed paint on them. They're kind of scary, like clowns sometimes are. There's a nurse, too. I'm unaware of what she does. And right now, the burning screen doesn't fit in. When his bones whistle, I imagine a skeleton in a dark corner of an attic. It seems to be a horror movie and now everything fits into place. In scary (terrifying) scenes, he holds her hands, they walk home after the movie in the snow and they hear the movie going on in the background, but it's not visible, just audible.

4. At first, the poem was unclear. I got two different impressions. The first paragraph was very vibrant with colors. The second paragraph changes the whole mood. It goes from color to black and white.

At second, the second paragraph stays the same and gets more colorful. It still doesn't make sense.

At third, it turns into a horror movie and everything seems to fit into place.

(Fourteen-year-old ninth grader)

Initially, Kim senses a contrast between "animated" and "colorless"; and being more engaged with the "animated," she imagines "a bright red car" and "a screen with red blood shooting through it." She says, ". . . it's like a . . . cartoon." Through re-reading, she imagines more details, transforming the cartoon of a red car and bloody screen into a "screen . . . on fire with flames" and a "huge pistol"—" 'technicolor' objects . . . on a comic page." When in her third reading Kim imagines "a drive-in movie," she begins to sense the "Reel One" situation; and eventually "a shoot out" at the drive-in becomes a "horror movie" on the screen. Kim's willingness to revise her initial organizing hypothesis, combined with the way she vividly imagines particular details, eventually brings her to a sense that "everything seems to fit into place." It was difficult for most of our young (eleven- and twelve-year-old) readers to develop a general sense of "Reel One" by inductively imagining it because they so often got lost in all the details that they were imagining; nevertheless, we hypothesize that *inductively imagining* is a powerful way of making meaning for more experienced readers.

Inductively Imagining and Explaining. Our most powerful readings—Charlene's (chapter 3), Vanna's (chapter 5), Nicole's and Jo Ann's (chapter 6), and Tanya's (chapter 7)—were created by readers *inductively imagining and explaining the situation.* Each of these readers—and they all were female—brought to life the general situation of a young man describing his experience of attending a violent movie in the company of a girlfriend and walking home afterward in the snow. Yet these young women brought their sense of the particular situation to life in their own ways, each imagining and explaining a somewhat different speaking voice and sensing to some degree her own voice in the situation. We are impressed and fascinated by the delicate balance between consensus and individuality among these memorable, confident, and rich readings of "Reel One." It is not possible, we hypothesize, to account for these readings by referring only to the features of the text or to the psychological makeup of the readers. What is required, we believe, is an understanding of how readers engage in a continuous dialogue between what is both socially shared and personally significant as they inductively imagine and explain their sense of the situation. In this way, these readers produce readings that are plausible and, at the same time, bear the stamp of individual concerns.

Meaning Making in and over Time

Although at any point it is possible to regard one's sense of the situation as *spatial,* we believe that it is more powerful to regard sensing the situation as *temporal.* As a temporal experience, meaning making and meanings evolve *in time* and *over time.*

Louise Rosenblatt has always spoken of meaning as a lived-through experience: "The poem, then, must be thought of as an event in time" (1978, 12). Patrick (chapter 4) vividly illustrates how readers can live through their imagined sense of a work:

> A guy watching a movie, horror, maybe 3-D. Colors seem amplified, guns shine brightly, and blood is redder. Explosion on the screen, he shivers in tension and fright. It all seems so real, but it's better than reality because it can't hurt him.
>
> He walks home with his girlfriend, he holds her hand tightly, no shadows to conceal killers, only the glaring white of the

snow. All is absolutely silent, so his overworked imagination makes voices out of the wind in the trees.

Here the goal is not to remember details in isolation or abstract a theme statement, but to experience the work of literature.

A more reflective *in-time* sensing of the situation occurs when readers are more aware of their moment-by-moment experiencing of the event (see Fish 1980, 21–67; Mailloux 1982, 66–92). We saw this, in part, as Nicole and Jo Ann (chapter 6) went about sensing and making sense of the voices of "Reel One." In addition, seventeen-year-old Evelyn captures her moment-by-moment experiencing of "Reel One":

> The author shows how modern technology applied to fiction often seems more real than real life.

After considering the power of the blood-and-guns imagery in contrast with the duller second-stanza imagery, she says:

> "Reel One" is an outcry against the way in which movies make "the real world" look dull and fake in comparison.

Then, after reflecting on how movies affect the way we see the real world, Evelyn says:

> But perhaps the author is trying to make a more general statement about how movies should not be compared to the real world, or else they distort one's sense of reality.

Finally, after thinking more about the second-stanza situation, she concludes:

> But, perhaps the fakeness of technicolor makes one appreciate the reality of what does exist, and helps one to maintain a true sense of what is.

If we were to assess Evelyn's readings from the perspective of how well they display the creation of a consistent interpretation, we might conclude that they are a failure. But if we assess Evelyn's readings from the perspective of *meaning as an in-time experience*, we can applaud her success; for clearly she has been living through some of the moment-by-moment thematic questions of "Reel One."

We might also regard meaning making and meaning as a temporal experience *over time*. What, for instance, would happen if we were able to assess how a reader's experiences with a text or an author changed as a result of several encounters at various points during that reader's life? Russell Hunt gives us one answer to that question:

> Now, there can be many Jonathan Swifts, just as there are many individuals in each of the people we converse with every day. My Jonathan Swift, this year, in the current situation of my own life, happens to be a passionate Irishman, who has things to say to me about the current troubles in Ulster and the Irish heritage of eastern Canada, where I now live. A few years ago, however, he was a skeptical Anglican rationalist, who spoke to me about my interests in the history of the Church of England and my wife's involvement in the Canadian Anglican church. Before that, he was a profoundly committed political and social conservative and journalist, with whom I argued about the political convictions with which I was struggling, and about which I was writing. At the very beginning, he was a childlike fantasist who (as Dr. Johnson put it) "thought of big men and little men," and spoke to my fascination with science fiction and various kinds of logical extrapolation. (1991, 118–19)

And why did Hunt read Swift differently over the years? "In each case . . . the basis of my engagement—whether I was aware of it or not—was my reading Swift as though he were talking to me, as though he were trying to change my mind and my soul . . ." (119).

Empowered readers realize that meaning making is a temporal process. They enjoy experiencing a situation in time, and they are open to exploring a situation over time. And they know that their sense of any situation is always subject to change—through time.

Realizing One's Concerns

When we become engaged in a work of literature, we experience one or more of our concerns. And if we attend to those concerns that arise during the act of reading, they can empower our meaning making. Thus when Charlene (chapter 3) engages in "Reel One," she realizes a concern about movies as an escape; and by attending to that concern, she explores and comes to understand more fully her own situation and the situation of "Reel One." Similarly, when Nick (chapter 5) reads "Reel One" as about the powers of TV to dull our senses, and when Vanna (chapter 5) reads "Reel One" as about the powers of the imagination to heighten our senses, both readers—during the act of reading—are realizing and being empowered by one of their concerns. Concerns provide a major answer to the reader's *so what* question. When Tanya (chapter 7) initially reads "Reel One," for instance, she is unable to engage in the work, admitting: "I do not especially like this poem." But after she explores her own related experience and realizes her concern with violence, she is able to engage in "Reel One," now admitting: "I like the poem better after reflecting on it." Of course, being aware of one's concerns is more helpful than being unaware. Ted (chapter 7) is able to engage in "Reel One" without being as consciously aware as is Tanya of what concerns him about that situation. As he reads, however, he becomes more aware of his concern with being a detached observer and how it is influencing his reading. Thus, at the end of his readings, Ted concludes that perhaps he needs to read "Reel One" still another time, in order to sense more fully the *speaker's* concerns.

The concept of *concerns* first became a major part of our vocabulary several years ago when we read Gerald Weinstein and Mario Fantini's *Toward Humanistic Education:*

> Concerns are deeper and more persistent than interests. A person may have an interest (in, say, urban poverty) and yet not be concerned . . . . Moreover . . . concerns go beyond "feelings," which do not necessarily arouse the frustration or anxiety associated with concerns. . . .
>
> Concerns may be positive, of course, rooted in aspirations and desires that are seeking outlets. But all concerns are negative in the sense that they signify disequilibrium or incomplete satisfaction—the gap between reality and an ideal. (1970, 37)

When trying to understand why a group of science students was so interested in evaporating water, for instance, Weinstein and Fantini hypothesized that the students were not concerned with evaporating water, per se, but with something else. "Upon questioning the pupils, . . . we found that it was not evaporation as such that fascinated the class but, rather, a concern with change and permanence; they were saying, in effect, 'If water can disappear, can we?' " (37). When students' questions about a situation arise from a sense of themselves and their concerns, authentic meaning making occurs.

If human beings have concerns, where do they come from? We hypothesize that whenever we experience a situation in which we sense a "gap between reality and an ideal," we are apt to experience one or more concerns. These concerns may be as concrete and short-lived as "Will the dentist be able to repair this tooth?" or as abstract and long-lasting as "Will I know a life after death?" Some concerns are so common among numerous persons that they may be regarded as developmental, cultural, or national concerns. On the other hand, some concerns may be so persistent and particular to one person over time that they may take on the nature of what psychoanalytic critic Norman Holland calls an *identity theme*.[1] Overall, we hypothesize that: we develop concerns primarily as a result of social situations; we can have a potentially infinite number of different concerns over time; we can experience concerns from the past when we encounter related situations in the present; in any particular situation, we may experience one or two concerns as paramount; and we experience our concerns with varying degrees of awareness and understanding.

What happens when a student realizes concerns with a text that are different from the teacher's concerns? When Robert Scholes, professor of humanities at Brown University, was an undergraduate English major, he went to New York to see the Broadway production of Arthur Miller's *Death of a Salesman.* "I had gone to the play because I was taking a course in tragedy and my instructor had posed the formal problem of whether this modern play could possibly be 'tragic' in the technical, literary sense of the word" (1987, 72). And did Scholes view *Death of a Salesman* with the teacher's concerns about the formal nature of tragedy uppermost in his mind? "[W]hat happened to me was something completely beyond the formal questions raised by my teacher. Issues that were absolutely vital to me—to what I would do with my life—were suddenly raised in a way that required my absolute attention" (72). Why was Scholes's concern with "what I would do with my life" evoked when he saw *Death of a Salesman*? Scholes explains: "my father owned a small business which he expected me, as his only son, to enter after graduation and eventually own. He had spent most of his life as a salesman . . . . *Death of a Salesman* . . . I saw . . . as being about me and my father and the career choices that lay ahead of me" (71–72).

Relating his sense of the *Death of a Salesman* situation to his own situation, Scholes experienced one of his major concerns— "What I would do with my life"—which became the major focus of and power behind his interpretation of both his own situation and Miller's play. "My own predicament was writ large, and not only could I read it, I knew now that it was not just my personal problem but the problem of a whole class of people struggling for decent satisfying lives in a culture that lacked viable models of decency and satisfaction" (72). And how did Scholes's experience with *Death of a Salesman* help him attend to his concern? "After graduation, I actually went to work with my father, but I took my first opportunity . . . to find another path through life" (72). Making sense of a text and realizing one's concerns are not separate experiences. We become empowered as readers and persons when we can realize and explore our own concerns in relation to the concerns of others.

Being Self-Aware and Other-Aware

Realizing our own concerns during the act of reading is not a problem—provided that we are aware of how our own voices are contributing to the meaning making, and how they are different from the voices of others. When readers are not self-aware, however, they may become—as we saw in the previous chapter—either critical or immersed. How, then, do readers develop the ability to be aware of their own voices and situations as they attempt to understand those of others? We can see this happening even at the beginning of meaning making. When eleven-year-old Albert (chapter 2) writes, "I read it real carefully and wrote what I thought about it," he indicates to some degree that he recognizes his role in bringing the "Reel One" situation to life. David (also chapter 2) indicates a similar degree of self-awareness when he suspends his interpretation of "Reel One" to imagine a related situation drawn from his own experience. Here, at the very beginning of meaning making, it is clear that these readers are distinguishing between the experiences of others and their own experiences, a prerequisite for effective meaning making. We sense three phases in readers' abilities to understand more fully the situations of others and the situations of themselves.

During the first phase, *readers unreflectively accept or reject the experiences of others in relation to their own.* David (chapter 2) unreflectively *accepts* the experiences of another in relation to his own when he imagines the speaker walking home after having seen a movie and then recalls a related personal experience: "He was watching a color movie. . . . Then he left and started walking down Bullet Road to home so many miles away. . . . A few years back in Putnam Valley where I live, I went to the movie with a friend. . . ." Bonnie (chapter 8) unreflectively *rejects* the experience of another in relation to her own when she writes: "How could she feel that blood and terror are better than life itself the way life goes? She has her own thoughts, but I feel that life should be a pleasure with hard times and work but not all terror and bone chills." Unreflective other-aware and self-aware readers seem to be asking: What is this person experiencing? Do I experience that? Do I like that? Although assessing others' experiences in relation to one's own and recalling related experiences may not lead to what we might consider great revelations, we believe that such readers are achieving important insights as they realize how their own experiences are similar to or different from those of others. Furthermore, such sensing of self and others enables readers to realize that texts and life are not unrelated categories.

During the second phase of exploring others and oneself, *readers reflectively accept or reject others' experiences in relation to their own.* Charlene (chapter 3) reflectively *accepts* the experiences of another in relation to her own as she senses the speaker's situation in "Reel One" and then concentrates on depicting and defining her own related situation: the various *holes* in her life, her habit of running from boring reality to heightened reality, her various complex emotions ("half-relieved," "half-saddened," "dread, stillness, ecstasy"), and her awareness of how she is postponing things. Through the process of reflecting, Charlene is understanding more fully how her movie experiences and her after-movie experiences are both related, yet different. Nicole and Jo Ann (chapter 6) focus reflectively on the experiences of another as they try to understand what the speaker in "Reel One" is feeling and thinking, and why. Reflective other-aware and self-aware readers seem to be asking: What is the nature of the experience? What are we feeling and thinking? When and how do we experience these things, and why? Unlike unreflective readers, who tend to concentrate on the surface features of what is going on, reflective readers try to understand the inner thoughts, feelings, and motivations of those involved in what is happening.

During the third phase of exploring others and oneself, *readers reflexively think about their thinking and meaning making in relation to their sense of others.* Tanya (chapter 7) demonstrates this when she not only recalls and reflects on her love of violent movies but *thinks about her thinking*: "For me, watching movies like that is a dual experience. In my logical, moral mind I know that war is a horrible thing, and messes up people's minds as well as their bodies, and I'd hate to be in a situation like that. But even a film like *Full Metal Jacket* which sets out to show how abominable and dehumanizing war is, gets you excited." Distinguishing between the two voices in herself enables her to distinguish between the author and the speaker in her sense of "Reel One." Ted (chapter 7) not only thinks about his thinking, but thinks about his meaning making: "I think I may have changed my meaning of the poem by identifying the narrator with myself rather than myself with the narrator. . . . Perhaps I should have placed myself in the poem instead of pulling the narrator out." Reflexive other-aware and self-aware readers seem to be asking: How are my own experiences, values, thoughts, concerns, and beliefs contributing to the way in which I am sensing the situation? And how are my meaning-making processes affecting the way in which I am sensing this situation? We agree with Jonathan Culler when he writes: "Instead of attempting to legislate solutions to interpretive disagreements, one might attempt to analyze the interpretive operations that produce these disagreements" (1981, 49).

There is no question in our minds that being self-aware and other-aware are critical aspects of empowerment. And the two understandings, we hypothesize, are related: we cannot be aware of our own situation in isolation from the situations of others, and we cannot really understand another's situation without being able to distinguish it from our own. This is why we suggest that all meaning making involves situating ourselves as we situate others. This is what happens in the best of conversations—where there is a mutual sharing of experiences and perspectives from which all participants come to respect and perhaps understand their similarities and differences more fully. And we sense that this is what happens in all reading situations where we are powerfully influenced by what we are reading. We find it unfortunate, however, that so many teachers do not allow students to reflect on their related experiences during the act of reading about the experiences of others.

How might we enable readers to be more self-aware and other-aware? First, we believe readers can benefit from sharing their various senses of the situation and reflecting on their ways of making meaning. Initially, it might be wise to see how readers, on their own, describe what they are doing. Then, it might be useful to introduce students to some of the concepts that we have been discussing in this book. The goal, of course, is not to have students memorize another set of labels, but to enable students to use multiple ways of making meaning, and to know how, when, and why each might be used.

A second approach for helping students to become more self-aware and other-aware is to introduce them to the concept of *concerns* and to explore how these naturally come into play as we engage in meaning making. Obviously there are many different ways for enabling students to do this: students might try to be more understanding of the concerns of particular persons in their lives; they might explore what seem to be the concerns of particular social groups, communities, or nations; and they might share what seem to be the concerns behind their different readings of the same text. Ultimately, being aware of how one's own concerns in a particular situation are related to and yet different from the concerns of others can become a natural part of every meaning-making event.

A third way of helping readers to become more self-aware and other-aware is to enable them to enhance their meaning making and meanings by moving into the worlds of professional writers, scholars, and critics—their strategies and terminologies, their multiple and interrelated texts, and their cultural and historical situations and traditions. We sense, however, that it is counterproductive to introduce these professional concerns before students have had the opportunity to fully experience and explore their own concerns.

The Element of Risk

We want to emphasize that the path to empowered reading involves risk. Encouraging students to reveal and explore with others their authentic concerns requires trust, patience, and a belief that those evoked concerns are of value. All too often, in our efforts to initiate students into the world of literary history and analysis, we ignore readers' concerns. Thus we may consume hours of class time dealing with issues that have little relationship to students' present situations.

An experience that one of us recently had dramatizes the nature and extent of this problem. As part of an inservice workshop, the purpose of which was to develop strategies for teaching specific novels, a group of teachers agreed to write in a journal as they read *Frankenstein.* The teachers opted for an open-ended format that permitted individuals to determine what and how to write as they went along. One of the most deeply moving journals was written by a recently divorced woman who wrote extensively about her empathy for the monster's expressions of pain caused by his being alienated and rejected. She said, in essence: "That's how I feel. Not only has my husband left me, but our mutual friends are hating me. I feel like a nonperson. I feel that there is no one in my life who cares about me. I feel horrible." What a powerful basis from which to explore Mary Shelley's novel. But what did the group of teachers do when they heard this woman's courageous sharing of these evoked concerns? They rushed on, seeking to know how to identify and pre-package knowledge about the literary devices and themes that they wanted to give to their students.

What is at risk when we ignore the concerns that arise as a part of our own reading situations? And what is at risk when we ignore the concerns that arise as a part of the reading situations of our students?

Note

1. Norman Holland describes Heinz Lichtenstein's concept of the *identity theme:* "for every individual there is a central identity 'theme' on which he lives out variations. . . . This invariant, when perceived in our encounter with another individual, we describe as the individual's 'personality'—or 'myth' or 'humour' or 'character' or 'ego identity' or 'lifestyle'. . . or 'identity theme'" (1975, 56–57).

10 How Might We Empower Readers in Our Classrooms?

There are many definitions of *empowerment,* and probably all teachers believe that they are empowering their students as readers in one way or another. Furthermore, there is no approach to reading and literature that does not neglect something that someone might consider important since no approach can emphasize everything. Finally, there is no approach to teaching and learning that is right for all teachers and all students at all times. Everything that we do in classrooms depends on how we read the situation; and that situation involves what those outside our classrooms are demanding, what our students expect and are able to handle, and what we as individual teachers value and are able to do. Thus teachers who guide students to a preferred reading of a class text, teachers who let students respond to a class text in any way they wish, teachers who have students read workbooks in order to learn how to answer multiple-choice questions, teachers who enable individual students to read anything they wish for whatever purpose, teachers who strive to give students an understanding of authors and literary history, and teachers who have students learn rhetorical terminology in order to label the elements of texts—all these teachers are doing what they know how to do and what they believe is valuable for students. And all of these teachers may be looking, as we have, for even better ways of empowering their students; for during the course of our forty-four combined years of teaching, we have been all of these teachers, and we have found each approach lacking.

What we wish to share with you, therefore, is not a definitive claim about how to empower readers in all classrooms, but some of the ways that we are trying in order to empower readers in our classrooms. We call the three-step, meaning-making process that is the basis for our curriculum in reading and literature *engaging, enhancing,* and *evaluating.* The goal of *engaging* is to enable students to read the text as rapidly and naturally as possible for the purpose of sensing the general situation and articulating some first impressions of it. The goal of *enhancing* is to enable students to realize their questions and concerns with the work and to explore one or more of those questions and concerns by re-reading portions of the text (and related texts, where appropriate) for the purpose of attending to the particular situation and voices of the situation. And the goal of *evaluating* is to enable students to review their enhanced senses of the work—their temporal experiences, their explorations of self and others, their dialogical insights—and to reflect on their successes and frustrations, their meaning-making processes, and their next steps for reading and learning.

Engaging

In the past, we engaged students in reading a text by giving them background information on the author and times, teaching lists of difficult vocabulary from the text, telling students what a great work they were about to read, and setting purposes for their reading. At the time, all of this seemed useful and necessary; in retrospect, we sense that our approach was too manipulative. Now we seek to do as little as is necessary to engage students in reading. For students who cannot read the text on their own, we read it—in part, orally—in class. For experienced readers who are used to reading long texts on their own at home, we just assign the work *in toto*—with next to no comment. For readers in between, who can and will read at home but who need some help getting started, we use a variation of what Margaret Meek Spencer calls *tuning the text* (1983, 72–83). When we worked with Steinbeck's *Of Mice and Men*, for instance, we had students read the first few pages and then share and explore what they sensed was going on. Students were surprised by how much of the *Of Mice and Men* situation they were able to sense by attending imaginatively and reflectively to the first couple of pages. They felt that the watering hole was somehow special and might be returned to later in the story. They hypothesized who George and Lennie were, why they were together, and where they had come from. And they predicted where George and Lennie might be going and what their futures might be. Enabling students to realize that they do not need to know about the author or the times or the meanings of unfamiliar words or what to look for—before they begin reading a text—is empowering.

The other aspect of engaging students is enabling them to articulate their first impressions. Several years ago, when we first became interested in student responses, we followed the advice of a then-popular book by having students express their responses in such creative ways as collages, drawings, and letters to the characters and author. The resulting responses were vivid and powerful, but we found that they were so final that students did not want to regard them as tentative and subject to revision. We abandoned that approach and, instead, had students write reading logs. But, again, the logs became so extensive that when we asked students to share them and learn from the writings of others, discussions were more defenses of first impressions than explorations toward new understandings. Then we decided to focus on the power of questions as a way to identify what students might explore next. So students brought in lists of questions about their sense of the work; but too often the students produced teacher-type questions in which they were not genuinely interested.

Now we believe that students' initial responses are most useful if they are short and honest, and if they reveal the readers' concerns. To obtain such helpful first impressions, we now ask three questions: (1) Without hesitating, what three things pop into your mind as you think back on the reading you have just done? (2) What thoughts and feelings do you have about the work? (3) What does the work remind you of? To accomplish this we have found that it is necessary to establish and sustain an atmosphere of trust in which everyone can feel comfortable in sharing their first impressions without censure or evaluation, for our overall rule about first impressions is that *they cannot be wrong.*

Once students have recorded their first impressions, they need time to sort through those initial responses and to explore what such responses might mean. One approach is to have students meet in small groups to share their first impressions and determine whether there are any issues toward which most of the group members gravitated. Then each group reports its findings to the whole class, the findings are put on the blackboard or are photocopied, and students can then determine which of the identified concerns they wish to explore, in what order, and how. Another approach, of course, is to have students share their first impressions with the entire class. The value of small-group sharing, however, is that it enables more students to talk at once, provides a filter for the selection of significant issues, and, in the long run, probably takes less time and produces more satisfaction for everyone than trying to deal with an entire classroom of voices at the same time. Once first impressions have been shared and constellations of concerns identified, it is time to go beyond first impressions—to *enhancing.*

Enhancing

Once readers have become engaged in imagining and explaining the general situation, they can move to asking questions about their developing sense of the particular situation. To see how this enhancing works, let us look at how three different classes of fourteen year olds sensed the general situation of Harper Lee's *To Kill a Mockingbird* and then went about exploring its particular situation.

The first class was composed of approximately twenty-five inner-city students. Throughout their in-class reading of the work as well as upon its completion, these students were most drawn to the situation of Boo Radley. What they wanted to explore in more detail were the following questions: Who is Boo Radley? What is he feeling and thinking throughout the story? What is his relationship to Scout, Jem, and Atticus? Why do people treat him the way they do? And why does he do what he does at the end of the story? So by re-reading those passages of the text dealing with Boo Radley and engaging in a series of activities designed to enhance their sense of that particular situation and voices, the students came to understand more about both Boo Radley and themselves. And what was the relationship between these students and Boo Radley? At first we could not understand why these students were focusing on Boo Radley. In all our years of teaching *To Kill a Mockingbird* to suburban students, we had never had any class be primarily concerned with Boo Radley. So why were these inner-city students so concerned? Slowly we came to realize that these students saw themselves as Boo Radley. Although much of the public regarded them as tough, potentially harmful beings, to themselves they were caring persons who were completely misjudged and being made invisible by society. So when they were exploring Boo Radley's situation, they were exploring their own. Here, for example, is what tough-looking Juan wrote about Boo Radley at the end of the unit:

Boo

I am a little child in a grown man's body
who wants to escape and be with somebody

I only come out at night when you are asleep
and put all I have in that old Radley tree

I live a lonely life that no one would like to live

in a dark world that is full of sins

To kill a mockingbird is one of them too
and no matter how mad I am that's something
I'll never do.

The second class was composed of approximately thirty-five semi-suburban whites who indicated at the end of reading the novel that they were primarily concerned with Atticus and his family: Atticus as a parent, the relationship between brother and sister, Dill's coming to visit, and the dislike of Atticus's relatives for the way in which he was raising the children. Since these students came from single-parent homes and/or homes with many children and/or situations where relatives came to visit or where they went to visit others, their explorations of the particulars of the Atticus Finch household were also explorations of their own situation.

The third group of students was quite similar in makeup to the second, but their first impressions were totally different. Initially, they expressed a fascination with the incident in which Atticus is called upon to shoot a rabid dog. First, they asked about the rabid dog and rabid animals in general. Second, they expressed confusion about the fact that Atticus at first resists taking the rifle and using it to fire the long-range shot that brings down the rabid dog. Why would a man who has the reputation of being "one-shot Finch" not want to fire the rifle? Third, upon re-reading that portion of the text, the students noticed for the first time that Atticus refuses to discuss with his son, Jem, both his marksmanship ability and how he acquired it. Why would a father who is an expert marksman not want even to talk about it or to demonstrate his skill with his son? Finding Atticus's behavior very odd in the rabid dog situation, the class began exploring in particular detail many of the other unusual aspects of Atticus: Why do his children address him by his first name? Why does he never say anything about his wife, the children's mother? Why does he wear a three-piece suit every day, even in 100-degree weather? And why does he underestimate the threat of Bob Ewell to his family? Linked together, these questions led the students to realize that Atticus was more human than Scout's adoring portrait seemed to suggest. And this insight led the students to explore Scout's role as a narrator and how views of adults can change over time. So by exploring their fascination with the rabid dog, Atticus's odd behaviors, and Scout as narrator, these students were also exploring their situations of trying to make sense of an adult world in which illness and evil are prevalent.

As fascinating as these three anecdotes might be, one still might ask, What do these students' explorations have to do with the major themes of *To Kill a Mockingbird*? After all, isn't that novel really about racial injustice in the U.S. South at a particular period in history, and isn't the trial of Tom Robinson at its center? Strange as it may seem, none of our many classes who have read *To Kill a Mockingbird* have ever focused on racial prejudice or the Tom Robinson trial as their point of concern. Yes, they understood that a great injustice had been done to this innocent black man; and, yes, they understood that racial prejudice and prejudice in general is a terrible thing. But after these understandings had been made public— and readers had little difficulty sensing these concepts—our students wanted to explore issues that were less obvious. Thus one class focused on Boo Radley, another on the Finch family, and another on rabid dogs and the oddities of an adult. What do these concerns indicate about how these students are sensing the situation of *To Kill a Mockingbird*? After all, if *mockingbird* is a metaphor for the preciousness of life, and if we should strive— as Atticus does—to not judge others but to walk in their shoes, then the thematic questions of *To Kill a Mockingbird* become: What is involved in walking in the shoes of another? What happens to people when they are unable to walk in the shoes of others or when others are unable to walk in their shoes? How is one to live in a world in which there are rabid animals that need to be killed? If these are some of the major thematic questions of *To Kill a Mockingbird*, then we believe these concerns are addressed by exploring the situation of Boo Radley—in whose shoes next to no one is able to walk; by exploring the Finch family relationships—all of which involve problems in being able to understand the viewpoints of others; and by exploring Atticus's reluctance to kill the rabid dog and to take the rabid Bob Ewell seriously—which involves Atticus's inability to attend to the darker aspects of nature and thus his inability to walk fully in the shoes of others.

What empowers students to move beyond their first impressions and to take responsibility for their own meaning making? A first step is providing students with the time and support that they require in order to generate their own questions, and then helping students determine what is important now for them based on their emerging concerns. Students' authentic questions are a powerful indication of what has been accomplished as well as what kinds of discussions and/or other activities might sustain a high level of engagement and learning. In all these efforts to enable students to enhance their first impressions, we believe that it is essential that students re-read those portions of the text directly related to their identified questions and concerns. Then by working individually or in groups—through one or more modes—students can explore and, ultimately, share their enhanced sense of the situation.

The most often used mode for enhancing students' readings is group discussion. Other modes that we have found useful, however, are listed in figure 3. These are not the only possible ways for enhancing our readings of a text, however; and we encourage you and your students to design whatever means seem most helpful for enabling students to explore more fully their text-related questions and concerns. Of course, there are lots of publications that recommend activities for livening up one's teaching; but many of these suggestions (e.g., "choose relevant events and construct a plot summary," "develop character sketches of the most important characters in each act," "build a replica of the Globe Theatre") are basically gimmicks—activities that a teacher can use to keep students occupied without having much understanding of what students are learning in the process. In contrast, we recommend that teachers and students collaboratively design enhancement activities that are (1) related to students' realized concerns, (2) engaged in only after students have re-read the related portions of the text; and (3) used to guide students toward being more other-aware and self-aware as they explore the more particular situation.

Evaluating

As our students assume increased responsibility for their own learning, we expect them to take an active role in setting goals and evaluating their progress. We seek to balance time devoted to negotiating curriculum with time devoted to reviewing and reflecting upon what has been accomplished, what has been learned. To facilitate these reflections, we require students to save in portfolios all their writings and other creations associated with their readings. Frequently we ask students to write and/or discuss with us their thoughts in response to such questions as: What have I been trying to accomplish by doing these particular readings, re-readings, writings, conversings, and other activities? What am I now able to do that I wasn't able to do in the past? And what do I seek to learn in the immediate future?

We do not have space to include an entire portfolio of several weeks of students' readings and writings, and students' reflections on them. But here is an example of one college undergraduate's enhancement activity for "Reel One." Roger took on the role of the girl, wrote

Enhancing Our Readings of a Text

The following enhancement activities are most successful if based on a re-reading of key parts or all of the text.

1. Perform your sense of one or more situations of the work:

   a. Create still-life portraits (tableaux) of your sense of one or more of the particular situations of the work.

   b. Improvise—or write and enact in your own words—your sense of one or more of the particular situations of the work.

   c. Dramatize your sense of the exact words of one or more of situations of the work (most appropriate for poetry and plays).

2. Experience your sense of one or more voices of the work:

   a. Prepare for and then allow yourself to be interviewed as one of the particular characters/persons of the work (hot seating).

   b. Interview—in writing—a particular character/person of the work (dialogue).

   c. Write what you sense to be a particular character/person's thoughts and feelings at a particular time (monologue).

3. Explore the work from another perspective:

   a. Imagine one or more portions of the work from another point of view (e.g., What if a different person had told the story? What if the point of view were more omniscient or less omniscient?).

   b. Imagine aspects of the work not presented by the author (e.g., What if the lives of minor characters had been developed? What if additional scenes and/or characters were added?).

   c. Translate your sense of the work into a different genre (e.g., capture the major events, characters, and thematic questions of a novel in a newspaper format; transform a short story into a play or comic book; translate a poem into a collage or song; re-create an essay into a dramatic discussion or debate).

Figure 3. Sample activities for enhancing students' readings.

a monologue to gain a better understanding of the girl's particular situation, and then recorded his reflections on that enhancement experience:

> Well, he took me to another one of those gory war movies. Can't he tell I hate them?! Whenever someone got shot, he grabbed my hand and squeezed it so hard I thought he'd break every one of my bones. Well, anyway, after the movie I wanted

to talk about something else—like maybe something *I* was interested in. He wouldn't even listen to me. I tried everything to get him to talk to me about something *real*, but all he wanted to do was walk in the snow. Have you ever tried walking in the snow in a skirt and heels? I was wet and cold and he didn't even care. He just kept staring at the trees like he was waiting for them to talk to him, or something. Maybe it's time to tell him how I feel.

I have never really written anything from a woman's point of view. In writing the monologue I tried to step into that woman's (girl's) heels and walk a mile through the snow in them after sitting through two hours of blood and guts. I had to examine such things as would she like the movie, what about the hand holding, and the snow, and the walk in silence. I went back to my own experience and recalled a conversation I had with an ex-girlfriend I used to take to hockey games on a regular basis. She hated them—but never told me—waiting for me to catch on. And one day I said, "You don't really like hockey, do you?" Wow, was she relieved—finally she could share what she really felt. That's why I wrote the last line—"Maybe it's time to tell him how I feel." If more people communicated their feelings, there might be less divorce, and probably less marriage as well.

Our ability to empower students to evaluate their own learnings through the use of portfolios and individualized self-reflection did not occur overnight. For many years we used short-answer tests and composition questions to evaluate what students had gained from our literature classes. But had we known about and been helped to implement early on other ways of evaluating learning, we believe that we would have made this transition more easily and speedily.

An example of a first step that teachers might take toward empowering students to evaluate their own learning in relation to literature can be seen in the experience of one of our student teachers, Valerie Walsh. After having taught *A Tale of Two Cities* to a group of advanced ninth-grade readers, Walsh gave students the typical test consisting of ten matching items (worth thirty points) and a composition question (worth seventy points). Almost all these gifted students received full credit for the ten matching items, and most did extremely well in the writing. Here, for example, is Ivan's answer to the following composition question: "Choose one character in *A Tale of Two Cities*, and examine that character's development and change within the novel. Do you find this character's change believable? Why or why not?"

> One character that changed in the novel is Sydney Carton. He changed from an unemotional man with no friends to a compassionate man that will be remembered as a hero for years to come. This change is believable.
>
> When we first meet Carton we learn many things about him. We learn he's a drunk. He is forever in bars drinking. This is exhibited at various parts in the novel, specifically after the acquittal when he went out with Darney. We also learn he is a cold man with no compassion. This trait is exhibited in his handling of Jarvis Lorry in court and his handling of Charles Darnay at the bar. All these traits will change at the end of the novel.
>
> By the time the book ends we see Carton as a compassionate man who's a hero. He takes the place of Charles Darnay on the guillotine. He took the place out of love and friendship. He never exhibited either of these traits at the beginning of the novel. In fact, he himself stated that he cares for no man and no man cares for him. To show love and friendship is a total change.
>
> He did this for love. I believe it because a similar thing happened to me. A girl I liked didn't like the way I talked to her friends. The next day I changed the way I talked. I changed out of love and so did Carton.
>
> To conclude I believe Carton's change is possible because he did it out of love, just as I changed out of love. To change for love is realistic, and that is why I believe that Carton's change is believable.

Although a few of the test essays written by students in this thirty-five-member class were more insightful than this one, Ivan's is typical. And Walsh's experience in reading the set of essays was that—by the end of the thirty-fifth paper—they all sounded quite alike.

When Harold asked Walsh what might happen if she asked students to choose their own questions, concerns, or topics to write about in relation to *A Tale of Two Cities*, she accepted the challenge by giving students an overnight homework assignment in which they were asked to explore in writing any aspect of the novel that concerned them. Here is what the same student, Ivan, wrote:

Dear Mr. Carton,

I hope as you look down from heaven at us you can see this letter.

I want to apologize for everything I said to your face and behind your back about you. I totally misjudged you. I thought of you as a drunken bum who didn't care about anything except if he had enough money to buy some alcohol. Looking back I see you are a kind and compassionate person. I know that what you did wasn't for me but for Lucie but I appreciate it just the same. Your love for Lucie is commendable. I think that your scheme was ingenious. Your whole plan was flawless. You knew you had to drug me because you knew I wouldn't go along. Then you knew that Madame Defarge wanted to kill my wife so you had to get them out of the country quick. You are an exceptional man and I will never forget what you did for my family.

Very truly yours,

CHARLES DARNAY

And what did Ivan think about these two writings—the teacher-specified composition and his own chosen essay?

I preferred the writing I did on my own. I discussed in the writing we did at home something that I felt was important. I discussed an issue that I felt needed to be addressed. In the test I felt the point we argued was dull. I could write about it from an intellectual point of view but it wasn't a writing that came from the heart. I didn't feel strongly either way about that dull issue.

I felt I did better on the free writing because I wrote about something that means something to me. I felt strongly about the point. I didn't have to think about it. It just flowed out. In the test it was a chore.

Another student, Marion, also chose to write about Sydney Carton for the test, concluding by arguing a position somewhat different from Ivan's:

I don't think that Carton ever really goes through a change. He is still the insecure person he was in the beginning of the book.

But by the end of the book, he makes that fateful decision to die for Lucie, proving once again that love does prevail over all.

For her own-choice writing about *A Tale of Two Cities*, Marion also chose to write about Sydney Carton, but in a way quite different from the teacher-formulated composition:

> Whenever I think of Sydney Carton, I think of this kid I used to know named David. He used to be in my class in my old school, and the truth was that no one really liked him. He was really quiet, and when he did say anything, it was usually something really off the wall. Kind of like Carton, only weirder. I couldn't stand him, because he really was unfriendly. But now my view of him has changed a little. Maybe he was nice. Maybe he just had a hard time expressing himself, like Sydney. Maybe he had good intentions, deep down. And now I think, would he have done something nice for me, even something unimportant, the way Carton did for Lucie? Probably not, and I wouldn't blame him. I feel guilty. I should've been nicer when I had the chance, you know.

Which of these two writings did Marion prefer?

> Personally I liked the freewrite better than the test composition. I liked writing about what I felt like writing about, as opposed to something that I *had* to write about. This is the kind of thing that I think about when I think about this book. I know that it's weird, but I think that that's what literature should do for you—make you think about how *your* life relates to the lives of the characters, and how you can make yourself a better person after learning about them.

The vast majority of the students in this class said they preferred the writing that they had chosen for themselves, though many questioned whether it would be worthy of a good grade. For us, the results of Valerie Walsh's experiment illustrate clearly the values of student-empowered explorations and evaluations.

If we enable students to evaluate their own abilities as meaning makers, what criteria might be used? The usual approach to evaluation is to determine a text's meaning and then see how well students are able to produce or re-produce that desired interpretation. But throughout this book, we have been suggesting that *meaning* is not a product, but an ongoing process: *a temporal experience of sensing and making sense of situations, an exploration of others and oneself.* What criteria, then, might we help students use to evaluate their abilities to sense and make sense of situations, others, and themselves over time? If readers are able to live through some of the work's thematic questions, and if readers are able to sense more of the work's situation and voices upon multiple readings, then these readers are learning the processes of experiencing meaning over time. And if, over time, students are more reflective and reflexive about what they are doing, then they are learning to be more responsible meaning makers.

But what if students seek *right answers*? What if they are not happy with being unable to attain, for all time, a complete understanding of the work? What if they do not like the fact that readers can have so many different interpretations? To address these concerns, we would try to help students develop the understanding that we are born in the midst of the conversations of humankind; and when we die, those conversations will still be going on.[1] One reason human conversation never stops, of course, is that most of the texts in our lives—nature, other people, ourselves—are continually changing. Thus we constantly need to make sense of those changes—so that we can decide what to do next. But what about the texts in our lives that remain the same over the years, such as words on a page? Can we interpret written texts once and for all and then stop talking about them? Not really—because words on the page are unable, by themselves, to contain and proclaim their meanings; because people are continually creating new lenses for interpreting the world; and because texts take on different meanings as people in different situations and at different times in their lives read them. Thus the conversations of humankind—even about the meaning of written texts—can never really be terminated.

If the ultimate meanings of texts cannot be determined, what are we to do? We can despair that human communication is inadequate, and curse the stupidity of our endeavors. We can accept certain persons' interpretations as authoritative and ignore or denounce all the rest. We can strive to make human communication more adequate by trying to define more clearly our procedures and codes for encoding and decoding meaning. We can accept, as Mailloux does in his *Rhetorical Power,* that meanings are always open to further interpretation; we can realize that all interpretations are historically and rhetorically determined; and thus we can argue for the interpretations in which we believe (1989, 133–49). Or, as we speak up for our views, we can also strive to be respectful of and understanding of the views of others. Of course, if we are not careful, our own pluralistic vision can become so precious and powerful that we may end up condemning all those who do not share our perspective. Thus, regardless of how hard we strive to see beyond our own situation, we are always potentially trapped by it—unless, of course, our situation includes lots of others and lots of dialogue.

Ultimately, therefore, if we are to regard meaning as a process, we also have to regard meaning as a *continuing conversation.* And how might we assess progress in meaning as an ongoing dialogue? If we regard reading as the act of having temporal experiences and exploring the situations of others and ourselves as part of those experiences, then progress can be determined by the number of voices with whom we are able to have a dialogue, the degree to which we realize that the *It* of any text can never be fully understood, and our willingness to continue participating in the conversations of humankind.

Empowering Students and Teachers

In approaching reading as a three-step process, we are trying to avoid what we experienced as students and what still happens in many classrooms: the practice of having students interpret the *particular* situation of a work before they have made sense of its *general* situation, and the practice of having students attend to *all* the particulars of a work. In this too-typical approach, the teacher has the class attend to the work chronologically, section by section, and interpret the particulars of each section as fully as possible. Teachers do this, we hypothesize, because they want students to get the fullest understanding of the work possible, and because they are unfamiliar with any other way to teach meaning making. From the students' perspective, however, such an approach is problematic. True, some students may appreciate this section-by-section explication, wanting instant answers to their questions and seeking to know the teacher's interpretations in preparation for the usual end-of-reading exam. For most students, however, section-by-section, chronological, in-depth analysis is murder. Why? First, asking students to deal with the particular aspects and voices of a work before having sensed the general situation is an impossible task. Second, this approach to reading gives students a totally false picture of the actual, trial-and-error, exploratory, recursive nature of meaning making. And third, the emphasis on numerous particulars without an overall sense of the situation to contain them, or a student-motivated reason for attending to them, leaves the work in an easily forgotten morass of minutiae.

That is why we are recommending the approach described in this chapter. By enabling students to get an overall sense of the work as rapidly as possible—by reading it themselves and not being told about it—and by enabling students to realize how the work concerns them, we then have a solid foundation from which to explore the particular situation and voices of the sensed work. By allowing students to choose those sections of the work to be explored, by understanding that all particulars of a work cannot be adequately addressed, and by realizing, along with Stanley Fish, "that what will be called the basic experience of a work (do *not* read basic meaning) occurs at every level" (1980, 41), we enable students to enhance their understanding of the work in a helpful and meaningful way. Finally, by enabling students to demonstrate what they have learned and to reflect on their ways of meaning making, we enable students to celebrate their growth, to assess their strengths and weaknesses, and to define their objectives for future learning.

We have been able to share only a portion of our ideas about teaching, but enough to let you know how we regard the situation. Although we have been talking primarily about reading and literature, in our teaching we try to interrelate all the language arts and to give students as much choice as possible. We want students to understand that learning and living are a matter of making choices, and we want them to be empowered to make those choices.

Our present approach to empowering students frees us to redirect our energies from predetermining and directing students' interpretations to understanding and empowering students' meaning making. Of course, we do not have the sense of control that we once had, we need to have greater patience as our students explore their initial impressions and try to realize their major concerns, and we need to have greater faith that our students will profit as much from their own meaning making as they might have from ours. But the fact is that this new way of teaching not only empowers our students; it also gives us a new lease on teaching. We are continually enlightened by our students' experiences with a work; we are learning about meaning making; and we are feeling rewarded as students remember the works that they have read, know how to make sense of other texts, and leave our classrooms wanting to read more.

If students were empowered readers in our classrooms, then no student would ever have to think what one of our graduate students thought when reflecting on her previous experiences in school:

> In my own experience, I have lived through many years of being an invisible reader. Many of my teachers were stuck on themes, literary devices, time periods, and who did what to whom. Not too many teachers asked me what my feelings were about a given work, and why I might be feeling that way. I see this as very unfortunate because I used to be a very involved reader, very sensitive to books, and I absolutely loved to read. I experienced books very strongly and so many had a powerful impact on my mind. It seems that many teachers are afraid to venture from more superficial questions and delve into the relationships that young readers develop with texts: What ideas are being evoked, what feelings, what conclusions, if any? It's such a waste of time to ask silly questions that don't engage the reader.

Note

1. For a similar conception, please see Kenneth Burke (1941, 110–11). For this reference to Burke's fable of society's conversation, we thank Steven Mailloux (1989, 56).

IV Conclusion

11 Continuing Reflections

Throughout *Situating Readers* we have been developing a theory of meaning making based on the hypothesis that reading is a process of sensing and making sense of situations. Being situated, we believe, encompasses much more than merely possessing appropriate linguistic and other cultural knowledge. To be situated is to be aware of ourselves engaged in experiencing a particular situation, at a particular time, with particular other people, and with particular purposes in mind, realizing that our sense of this particular situation is potentially influenced by all the previous voices and experiences that affect how we interpret the world and how we see ourselves. Thus, for instance, each member of the same social group experiencing a familiar cultural situation may share a common sense of its general nature, yet have a different sense of its particular meaning. These social and personal aspects of meaning making ought to be acknowledged, we believe, as integral—not peripheral—to a clear understanding of what people do when they read.

Throughout this book, we have been exploring these social and personal aspects of meaning making. In fact, the concepts that we discuss are the result of extensive and ongoing revision. Originally, we attempted to categorize readings on the basis of a generalized and decontextualized notion of what actual readers do. But in our efforts to attend closely to our students' experiences with "Reel One," we were amazed by their variety and *situatedness*. As we struggled to make sense of these student interpretations, therefore, we were forced to acknowledge that the social and personal dimensions of reading are much more significant than we had imagined.

The theory of meaning making that we have been developing throughout this book is, of course, neither totally our own nor the final word. Though we believe that our efforts have enhanced the ongoing conversation about how readers make sense of texts, writing this book has generated additional questions and concerns. We end this research, therefore, by identifying some of the major issues that we have begun to explore, and we invite your participation as we seek to enhance our understanding of readers and their situations.

Readers and Reading

Since the days when we felt bewildered by our students' readings of "Reel One," we have worked through many problems, revised our thinking, and arrived at several insights. But some questions and concerns remain about readers and their reading.

Enhancing Reading

Our research has guided us toward a better understanding of what readers (especially young readers) do when they read, what is disempowering for them, and what is empowering. We now know that being unable to sense a situation, being critical or immersed, and being preoccupied with abstracting theme statements are disempowering acts of reading. We have learned, also, that inductively imagining and explaining the situation, attending to one's own and others' concerns, and being self-aware and other-aware are empowering meaning-making strategies. Our questions now center on classroom practices and how well they enhance the reading experiences of our students. Which enhancing activities are most helpful for which meaning-making concerns? How might we better decide when to focus on individualized learning and when to encourage collaboration? And how can we become more adept at recognizing *what is important now* for students in our classrooms?

Resistant Reading

Since our population of readers consisted of mostly white, middle-class students, and since the situation that most of our readers brought to life as they read "Reel One" was thought-provoking without being provocative, the concerns that our readers raised did not embroil them or us in major issues of *gender, class, religion,* or *race.* But what if a different population of readers or a different text had emphasized one or more of these issues? We raise this question because we have been hearing a lot of talk lately about the concept of the *resisting reader* (Fetterley 1978; Corcoran 1990). According to this concept, empowerment is associated with becoming sensitized to prejudicial and oppressive ways of reading that can influence readers without their even being aware. Some advocates of resistant reading assert that students should be taught to be alert for ways that authors and their texts manipulate and even silence readers: "Our 'real-life' experience is never determined by others to the extent that our reading is determined by authors" (Medway and Stibbs 1990, 77). While we would agree that readers can have powerful experiences with authors' texts, our research makes us resistant to the notion that authors and their texts, in and by themselves, possess the power to manipulate readers. Instead, we would argue that ways of seeing and experiencing arise as a consequence of how readers situate themselves.

The antidote to oppressive or prejudicial ways of reading lies in helping readers develop a questioning and reflective other-aware and self-aware stance. This is what many of the readers in our research did. In sensing and accounting for the "Reel One" situation, for instance, our readers responded to the line "It was like life, but better" by asking: Is "It" the subject matter of a particular movie, or movies in general, or the total experience of watching a movie in a theater with a girl? And what kind of person would make such a claim and why? Questions like these prompted others: How do I think moviegoing and life are similar, dissimilar? Under what circumstances might I assert that movies are like life, but better? And some of our readers wondered about the girl: How might her account of the situation have differed from that of the speaker? Clearly, these readers are not acting like passive consumers of the author's or the text's meaning making.

We hypothesize that readers who are empowered—who feel free to explore their own questions and concerns—will engage in reflective and reflexive thinking. Does this mean that they are being resistant readers? And this question leads to others: What are the various roles open to readers as they make sense of texts? To what extent is a particular role dependent upon a reader's initial engagement with a text or upon the teacher's perspective? Can the role of the reader shift during the course of a reading event? What empowers a reader to shift roles? How does taking on multiple roles affect the quality of a reader's experience? And is being resistant the ultimate aim of reading?

Connected Reading

A striking aspect of our collection of readings is that the overwhelming majority of our most empowered readers were female. While this may be explained, in part, by the fact that most of our readers were under eighteen years of age, we do not think this accounts for the clear differences that we observed. Females, we discovered, are much more likely than males to engage in what Belenky et al. (1986) call "connected knowing," and this significantly influenced the ability of each female to generate powerful, memorable reading experiences on her own.

In describing "connected knowing," Belenky et al. could well be describing many of our most empowered readers of "Reel One": "Connected knowing builds on the . . . conviction that the most trustworthy knowledge comes from personal experience rather than the pronouncements of authorities" (112–13). "Connected knowers develop procedures for gaining access to other people's knowledge. At the heart of these procedures is the capacity for empathy" (113). Connected knowers "engage in . . . energetic forms of listening . . ."; they "begin with an interest in the facts of other people's lives, but they gradually shift the focus to other people's ways of thinking" (114, 115). Like so many of our female readers, connected knowers "take naturally to a nonjudgmental stance" (116). And connected knowers do not come to understand others by the typical male way of projecting themselves into others: "In describing connected knowing the women we interviewed used images not of invading another mind but of opening up to receive another's experience into their own minds" (122). Trusting personal experience, empathizing with others, listening, being nonjudgmental, receiving another's experience—these are the ways in which our most empowered readers sensed and made sense of the situation.

Among the more exciting outcomes of our research is our newfound sensitivity to the possible relationship between gender and reading. Are females more inclined than males to be situating readers? If so, how can we nurture "connected knowing" in our classrooms so that *all* students might benefit from its power? And what are the similarities and differences between *resistant reading* and *connected reading*, and what are the relative merits of each?

Readers and Learning

In part three of this book, we explored how the concepts of part two might be applied to literature instruction in our classrooms. Now, an important next step would be to ask how these findings and recommendations might be useful in other learning situations.

Relating Reading and Writing

Our most empowered readers inductively imagined and explained the "Reel One" situation by writing about it. While this fact only corroborates now-familiar claims about the value of writing as a response to literature, we are intrigued by the more radical idea that both reading and writing experiences remain incomplete unless the two are integrated. Another way of putting this is to suggest that reading and writing, when pursued in tandem, produce a very different and more powerful experience than either activity is capable of producing on its own. If this is so, then in what ways can these two meaning-making processes—reading and writing—be interrelated so as to produce texts and knowledge that are more powerful and long-lasting than could be produced by either process alone? And to what extent might the meaning-making strategies that we have identified as enabling students to interpret the texts created by others be as empowering for students attempting to create their own texts?

Empowering All Students as Meaning Makers

Our research is based on attending to what many readers say about their experiences with a common text, a poem. Does this mean that our theory of meaning making is limited to the experience of poetry? We do not believe so. Of course, no one would argue with the statement that the experience of reading a poem differs in some ways from that of reading a novel, a short story, a play. Nevertheless, many reading theorists—including Louise Rosenblatt (1978), Iser (1976, 1989), and Stanley Fish (1980)—emphasize the essential similarity of the meaning-making process across literary genres.

What we find fascinating is the growing amount of evidence that meaning making as we are describing it could empower learning across the curriculum. We have known for some time now that all meaningful knowledge is in reality personal knowledge (Polanyi 1958) and that the most effective teachers are facilitators, rather than transmitters, of knowledge, even in science, math, and social studies classes (Barnes 1976). In addition, important work on the relationship between meaning making and language acquisition (Smith 1983; Wells 1986), meaning making and the role of narrative (Bruner 1986, 1990; Witherell and Noddings 1991), meaning making and multiple intelligences (Gardner 1983), and meaning making as the construction of knowledge in classroom settings (Newman, Griffin, and Cole 1989; Tharp and Gallimore 1988; Gardner 1991) suggests that *situated reading* is related to *situated learning*. How well, then, do the concepts that we have been discussing throughout *Situating Readers* support meaning making not only in the English classroom but throughout the school curriculum? And how well do the ways of meaning making that we discuss in *Situating Readers* describe and explain how readers make sense of nonliterary texts in the English classroom, make sense of nonliterary texts in other disciplines, and make sense of nonprint texts such as people, paintings, and movies?

Assessing and Evaluating with Portfolios

In *Situating Readers*, we have documented and explained how reading evolves *in time* and *over time*. Reading evolves in time from the very beginnings of meaning making to the complex reflective and reflexive thinking that many of our readers achieved during the course of three readings. Reading evolves over time as questions and concerns change with readers' advancing maturity. In light of this, we strongly believe that the practice of using quizzes, tests, and theme papers to evaluate learning creates a climate that fails to allow for the time and the experience of the process that young people need in order to develop into empowered and lifelong readers. In contrast, the practice of portfolio assessment and evaluation offers a powerful remedy. By enabling students to preserve and/or otherwise document their readings and writings in and out of the classroom, portfolios provide an answer to the *assessment* question, What did I do? In addition, portfolios enable students and teachers to step back and reflect upon the accumulated material, thus answering the *evaluation* question, What did I learn? Although much of the most recent discussion about portfolio assessment and evaluation focuses exclusively on writing (Belanoff and Dickson 1991; Yancey 1992), there are clear indications that the trend is toward classroom portfolios that embrace both writing and reading experiences (Wolf 1987/88; Valencia 1990; Tierney, Carter, and Desai 1991).

In addition to engendering a climate of respect for the temporal aspects of reading, portfolios can support efforts to achieve a number of other important goals associated with reading and learning. Portfolios can create a place for students to document what and when they are reading and to collect their own and others' responses to literature. Portfolios can assist teachers in encouraging students to listen to themselves and each other in ways that engender self-awareness about what they are able to do and what they hope to accomplish. And portfolios can help students feel a sense of ownership and develop a sense of responsibility for their own learning.

We believe that our research contributes to the growing evidence in favor of forms of assessment and evaluation that are more meaningful and useful for learners. But how well do the principles and practices that we propose enable students to assess and evaluate their accomplishments, frustrations, and development over time?

Readers and Society

In "The Background for Reform," Arthur Applebee notes "an important shift in what counts as knowledge, and by implication what should be taught in schools." With this shift:

> Instruction becomes less a matter of transmittal of an objective and culturally sanctioned body of knowledge, and more a matter of helping individual learners learn to construct and interpret for themselves. There is a shift in emphasis from content knowledge to processes of understanding that are themselves shaped by and help students to become part of the cultural communities in which they participate. (1992, 3)

We believe that our study supports this shift in emphasis, and we identify three areas of concern that we seek to understand more fully.

Reading and Voice

Throughout part two of this book, we have used the term *voice* to account for our sense of certain aspects of the reading process. Now, upon reflection, we would like to make explicit a relationship that we only partly realized: the relationship between our sense of the concept of *voice* and our sense of the concept of *concerns*. When Harold contrasted Patrick's reading with David's in chapter 4, for instance, he said: "Patrick attends to more of the author's words than do any of the readers we've looked at thus far.... David uses the author's words.... Yet the primary voice is his own." Here Harold is using *voice* to refer to David's focus on the loveliness of the after-movie experience. Certainly David's reading of the general situation of "Reel One" is supported by the text. But David's inattention to most of the author's words and his recollection of a personal experience so similar to his interpretation of "Reel One" now lead us to suggest not only that the voice is primarily David's but that this particular voice of David's emerged when his concern with quiet walks in the snow became situated during his reading of "Reel One."

In contrast with our sense of David's univocal reading is our sense of the complex set of voices that emerged during Tanya's reading of "Reel One." In chapter 7, Mark identifies the voices: "In her first reading she had identified two voices in herself—one fascinated by violence and the other decrying it. Now during her third reading, she senses two voices in the 'Reel One' situation—that of the speaker and that of the implied author." And what enabled these four voices to emerge? We now wish to emphasize that we believe these voices emerged because Tanya's reading of "Reel One" had engaged one of her concerns—her concern with violence. In exploring this concern, therefore, four voices were realized—one of Tanya's voices and the speaker's voice favoring the fascination for violence, and another of Tanya's voices and the implied author's voice speaking against violence. The complexity of Tanya's readings is directly related to her clear sense of these points of view regarding violence.

We are aware that the way in which we are using the concept of *voice* in relation to *concerns* is both uncommon and not as well developed as we would like it to be. But support for our line of reasoning is growing and sometimes can be found in unexpected places. In a recent issue of *American Psychologist,* for instance, Dutch researchers Hubert Hermans, Harry Kempen, and Rens van Loon write: "There is growing awareness among psychologists that the individualistic and rationalistic character of contemporary psychological theories of the self reflect an ethnocentric Western view of personhood. In opposition to this view, it is argued from a constructionist perspective that the self can be conceived of as dialogical . . . " (1992, 23). And what is the nature of the *dialogical self?*

> . . . we conceptualize the self in terms of a dynamic multiplicity of relatively autonomous *I* positions in an imaginal landscape. In its most concise form this conception can be formulated as follows. The *I* has the possibility to move, as in a space, from one position to the other in accordance with changes in situation and time. The *I* fluctuates among different and even opposed positions. The *I* has the capacity to imaginatively endow each position with a voice so that dialogical relations between positions can be established. The voices function like interacting characters in a story. Once a character is set in motion in a story, the character takes on a life of its own and thus assumes a certain narrative necessity. Each character has a story to tell about experiences from its own stance. As different voices these characters exchange information about their respective *Mes* and their worlds, resulting in a complex, narratively structured self. (28–29)

From this perspective, and ours, the self is a repository of potentially hundreds of voices, variously engaged in dialogue with one another as the *I* moves from one situation to another.

But not everyone regards the self in this way. In fact, most people in the Western world regard the self as a unified, disembodied, and individualized being that remains consistent throughout time and unaffected by history. It is this popular conception of self and its supposed embodiment in a singular, personal *voice* that Pam Gilbert argues against: "The concept of voice as the power that makes a text intelligible and readable is both an unhelpful and misleading explanation of how meaning is produced in discourse. Further, it is a disempowering concept for learners and teachers" (1991, 206). Instead of teaching that *personal voice* is the driving force behind powerful reading and writing experiences, Gilbert argues that we ought to help students become aware of the fact that all discourse is affected by the linguistic and sociocultural aspects of particular social situations. According to Gilbert, and we concur, teachers could be doing a lot more to demystify "the craft of writing" and "the practice of reading" in order to make more explicit "how *all* language practices are social practices" (209).

While we agree that students need to develop self-awareness about how they, and consequently their reading and writing, are situated within discourse communities, we are not convinced that the word *voice* needs to be abandoned. According to the Russian philosopher and critic Mikhail Bakhtin (1984, 1986), we ought to avoid implying that *voice* can ever be an attribute of a singular personality. A more useful way of thinking is to recognize *voices* as aspects of particular social situations. Normally, Bakhtin observes, we tend to think of voice as the outward expression of an inwardly residing personality. By reversing this inside-out formulation, Bakhtin claims that voices are inseparable from particular instances of dialogue in which two or more respondents realize their concerns. Bakhtin asserts that we can only *hear* ourselves speak when actively conversing with others, and that the sense each of us has of being a more or less stable self is of necessity continually being revised as we respond to the always-shifting demands of social situations.

We value these and similar arguments (see Holquist 1990) that contribute to an emerging theory of the *dialogical self.* On the basis of our own research and the research of others, therefore, we now hypothesize that *voice is a dialogical dimension of situated concerns.* In what ways, then, might this depiction of *voice* and *concerns* empower readers to make sense of the texts of others? And in what ways might it empower readers to create and understand their own texts?

Reading and Community

Although our students' interpretations of "Reel One" resulted, in part, from each reader's personal experiences and concerns, those readings also resulted from linguistic and sociocultural experiences shared by all our readers. All knew what it is like to go to a movie. All but our very youngest readers experienced no difficulty with the words *technicolor, screen, soundtrack,* and *reel.* They all had experienced violence in movies, so it was easy for them to imagine situations involving "guns," "blood," "bullets," and "nurses." Most of our readers had experienced going to a movie with a friend of the opposite sex. And the phrase "we walked home, after, / with the snow falling" made perfect sense to readers residing in the Northeast United States. These observations are so obvious that it is easy to forget how incomprehensible "Reel One" would be to someone who had never been to a movie, never seen violence, or never walked through snow with a friend.

What concerns us about the many readings that we gathered is not whether we can identify in broad strokes the relevant background experiences shared by our readers, but whether we can account for the communal as well as the individual aspects of these experiences. Is such a distinction between the communal and the individual even possible in any but a theoretical sense? James Wertsch's (1985, 1991) elaboration upon the work of Lev Vygotsky (1962, 1978) addresses these questions in a manner that seems promising to us because it emphasizes the social formation of mind. Also valuable are Clifford Geertz's (1983) concepts of *thick description* and *local knowledge.* In a sense, our dialogues in chapters 2 through 7 exemplify a type of *thick description* as we attempt to situate each reader of "Reel One" in relation to her or his own purposes and processes, not ours. As we continue to build on our theory of reading as a situated and a situating process, we hope to join the growing number of theorists and teachers who are committed to curricular reform based on social constructionist approaches to meaning making.

According to Kenneth Bruffee, "A social constructionist position in any discipline assumes that entities we normally call reality, knowledge, thought, facts, texts, selves, and so on are constructs generated by communities of like-minded peers" (1986, 774). While we acknowledge the power of this stance, we remain unsure about what exactly Bruffee and others mean when they talk about "communities of like-minded peers." Did our readers of "Reel One" constitute such a community? We suspect that their situation was much more complex and that, as Joseph Harris argues, only a very "specific and material" description of how people "share beliefs or practices with one another" can protect the term *community* from becoming just another "empty and sentimental word" (1989, 20, 13). How, then, might we better describe the sociocultural aspects of our students' meaning making? And in what ways are or could the students in our classrooms be regarded as one or more communities of meaning makers?

Reading and Democracy

In our view, *Situating Readers* joins with many of the works that we have cited in attempting to define and occupy what might be called a middle ground between two competing paradigms that currently define the goals of literacy in America. At one extreme are those who champion the well-established view of *cultural literacy* (Bennett 1984; Bloom 1987; Hirsch 1987), according to which all students should read the same set of desirable books and acquire the same kind of knowledge. At the other extreme stand the advocates of an equally well established *personal growth* metaphor for teaching and learning, according to which students should be assisted in doing and learning pretty much whatever they wish. We believe that both perspectives are too confining and lead to practices that fail to engender the kind of communal consciousness that could be both empowering and life-enhancing for our students. Our middle ground requires teachers to consider *what is and is not negotiable* in an English curriculum. On the one hand, students should be aware of what they need to know and need to be able to do if they are to be active and productive members of our society. On the other hand, there remain a variety of goals and activities that students can choose for themselves and a host of ways in which students can experience ownership and assume responsibility for their learning. Involving students, individually and collaboratively, in deciding what to do as a community of learners within the context of a classroom is the best way, we believe, to prepare them to live well within the larger community beyond school.

Writing in response to the remarkable English Coalition Conference which took place in 1987, Wayne Booth writes:

> After all, it is only when we teachers engage in reflection on what we want to learn and why, only when we "take responsibility for our own meanings," that we become models of what we want our students to become. Only if we lead our students to take such active responsibility will they become full participants in the political and cultural life they will meet after they leave our care. (1989, xii)

These concerns loom large for us as we reflect on the journey that has resulted in the publication of this book and has sensitized us in new ways to the importance of a host of authors whose works speak to the purposes of a literary education in our complex, multicultural society (Dewey 1938; Giroux 1988; Harris 1989; Mayher 1990; Pradl 1986, 1991; Wigginton 1985; Willinsky 1991). Our society can no longer support—if it ever could—a concept of literary education that is preoccupied with the business of literary criticism or the business of preparing all students to be readers of only a white, male, and Western canon of texts. Neither can we condone a program based only on assigned reading or only on independent reading. Being an empowered reader involves more than just reading well the texts chosen by someone else or the set of texts preferred by oneself. Empowered readers are capable of imagining, explaining, and *respecting* multiple ways of making sense of the world. So the question remains: Once we have begun to be aware of the many voices within and without ourselves, how will we situate them and how will we act?

Works Cited

Alexander, Max. 1989. "Once More, the Old South in All Its Glory." *New York Times*, January 29, p. H13.

Applebee, Arthur. 1992. "The Background for Reform." In *Literature Instruction: A Focus on Student Response,* ed. Judith A. Langer. Urbana, Ill.: National Council of Teachers of English.

Bakhtin, Mikhail. 1981. *The Dialogic Imagination: Four Essays.* Austin: University of Texas Press.

———. 1984. *Problems of Dostoevsky's Poetics.* Minneapolis: University of Minnesota Press.

———. 1986. *Speech Genres and Other Late Essays.* Austin: University of Texas Press.

Barnes, Douglas. 1976. *From Communication to Curriculum.* London: Penguin Books.

Beach, Richard, and Susan Hynds. 1990. "Research on Response to Literature." In *Transactions with Literature: A Fifty-Year Perspective,* ed. Edmund J. Farrell and James R. Squire. Urbana, Ill.: National Council of Teachers of English.

Belanoff, Pat, and Marcia Dickson, eds. 1991. *Portfolios: Process and Product.* Portsmouth, N.H.: Heinemann Educational Books.

Belenky, Mary Field, Blythe McVicker Clinchy, Nancy Rule Goldberger, and Jill Mattuck Tarule. 1986. *Women's Ways of Knowing: The Development of Self, Voice, and Mind.* New York: Basic Books.

Bennett, William. 1984. *To Reclaim a Legacy.* Washington, D.C.: National Endowment for the Humanities.

Benton, Michael, and Geoff Fox. 1985. *Teaching Literature: Nine to Fourteen.* Oxford: Oxford University Press.

Benton, Michael, John Teasey, Ray Bell, and Keith Hurst. 1988. *Young Readers Responding to Poems.* London: Routledge.

Berg, Temma. 1991. "Louise Rosenblatt: A Woman in Theory." In *The Experience of Reading: Louise Rosenblatt and Reader-Response Theory,* ed. John Clifford. Portsmouth, N.H.: Boynton/Cook.

Berger, Peter, and Thomas Luckmann. 1966. *The Social Construction of Reality: A Treatise in the Sociology of Knowledge.* New York: Doubleday.

Bleich, David. 1988. *The Double Perspective: Language, Literacy, and Social Relations.* New York: Oxford University Press.

Bloom, Allan. 1987. *The Closing of the American Mind: How Higher Education Has Failed Democracy and Impoverished the Souls of Today's Students.* New York: Simon and Schuster.

Booth, Wayne. 1974. *A Rhetoric of Irony.* Chicago: University of Chicago Press.

———. 1989. "Foreword." In *The English Coalition Conference: Democracy through Language,* ed. Richard Lloyd-Jones and Andrea A. Lunsford. Urbana, Ill.: National Council of Teachers of English.

Britton, James. 1982. "Shaping at the Point of Utterance." In *Prospect and Retrospect: Selected Essays of James Britton,* ed. Gordon Pradl. Portsmouth, N.H.: Boynton/Cook.

Bruffee, Kenneth. 1986. "Social Construction, Language, and the Authority of Knowledge: A Bibliographic Essay." *College English* 48 (8): 773–90.

Bruner, Jerome. 1965. *On Knowing: Essays for the Left Hand.* New York: Atheneum.

———. 1986. *Actual Minds, Possible Worlds.* Cambridge: Harvard University Press.

———. 1990. *Acts of Meaning.* Cambridge: Harvard University Press.

Burke, Kenneth. 1941. *The Philosophy of Literary Form.* Baton Rouge: Louisiana State University Press.

Caird, John. 1987. Quoted in Jeremy Gerard, "The Hunter and the Hunted." *New York Times,* March 8, pp. H1, H8.

Collingwood, R. G. [1938] 1958. *The Principles of Art.* Oxford: Oxford University Press.

———. [1946] 1956. *The Idea of History.* Oxford: Oxford University Press.

Corcoran, Bill. 1990. "Reading, Re-reading, Resistance: Versions of Reader Response." In *Reading and Response,* ed. Michael Hayhoe and Stephen Parker. Bristol, Penn.: Open University Press.

Culler, Jonathan. 1981. *The Pursuit of Signs: Semiotics, Literature, Deconstruction.* London: Routledge and Kegan Paul.

Dewey, John. 1938. *Experience and Education.* New York: Collier Books.

Dias, Patrick. 1987. *Making Sense of Poetry: Patterns in the Process.* Ottawa: Canadian Council of Teachers of English.

Donoghue, Denis. 1985. "Newton's Other Law: Glory Is the Real Reward." *New York Times Book Review,* April 21, p. 34.

Eagleton, Terry. 1983. *Literary Theory: An Introduction.* Oxford: Basil Blackwell.

Faust, Mark. 1990. "Reconsidering What We Talk about When We Talk about Literature: Social Constructionist Metaphors in Criticism and Teaching." Ph.D. diss., New York University.

Fetterley, Judith. 1978. *The Resisting Reader: A Feminist Approach to American Fiction.* Bloomington: Indiana University Press.

Fish, Stanley. 1980. *Is There a Text in This Class?* Cambridge: Harvard University Press.

Frye, Northrop. 1957. *Anatomy of Criticism: Four Essays.* Princeton: Princeton University Press.

Gardner, Howard. 1983. *Frames of Mind: The Theory of Multiple Intelligences.* New York: Basic Books.

———. 1991. *The Unschooled Mind: How Children Think and How Schools Should Teach.* New York: Basic Books.

Geertz, Clifford. 1983. *Local Knowledge: Further Essays in Interpretive Anthropology.* New York: Basic Books.

Gilbert, Pam. 1991. "From Voice to Text: Reconsidering Writing and Reading in the English Classroom." *English Education* 23 (4): 195–211.

Gilligan, Carol. 1982. *In a Different Voice: Psychological Theory and Women's Development.* Cambridge: Harvard University Press.

Giroux, Henry. 1988. *Schooling and the Struggle for Public Life.* Minneapolis: University of Minnesota Press.

Gussow, Mel. 1987. "Stage: The Roundabout Offers 'Of Mice and Men.' " *New York Times*, October 22, p. C24.

Harris, Joseph. 1989. "The Idea of Community in the Study of Writing." *College Composition and Communication* 40 (1): 11–22.

Hermans, Hubert, Harry Kempen, and Rens van Loon. 1992. "The Dialogical Self." *American Psychologist* 47 (1): 23–33.

Hirsch, E. D., Jr. 1987. *Cultural Literacy.* Boston: Houghton Mifflin.

Holland, Norman. 1975. *5 Readers Reading.* New Haven: Yale University Press.

Holquist, Michael. 1990. *Dialogism: Bakhtin and His World.* London: Routledge.

Hunt, Russell. 1991. "Modes of Reading, and Modes of Reading Swift." In *The Experience of Reading: Louise Rosenblatt and Reader-Response Theory*, ed. John Clifford. Portsmouth, N.H.: Boynton/Cook.

Iser, Wolfgang. 1976. *The Act of Reading: A Theory of Aesthetic Response.* London: Routledge and Kegan Paul.

———. 1989. *Prospecting: From Reader Response to Literary Anthropology.* Baltimore: Johns Hopkins University Press.

Kakutani, Michiko. 1989. "Books of the Times: Past Traced to the Present in a Family's Intricate Story." *New York Times*, October 20, p. C21.

Kintgen, Eugene. 1983. *The Perception of Poetry.* Bloomington: Indiana University Press.

Labov, William. 1972. *Language in the Inner City: Studies in the Black English Vernacular.* Philadelphia: University of Pennsylvania Press.

Lakoff, George, and Mark Johnson. 1980. *Metaphors We Live By.* Chicago: University of Chicago Press.

Langer, Judith. 1989. *The Process of Understanding Literature.* Albany: Center for the Learning and Teaching of Literature, State University of New York at Albany.

Mailloux, Steven. 1982. *Interpretive Conventions: The Reader in the Study of American Fiction.* Ithaca: Cornell University Press.

———. 1989. *Rhetorical Power.* Ithaca: Cornell University Press.

Mayher, John. 1990. *Uncommon Sense: Theoretical Practice in Language Education.* Portsmouth, N.H.: Boynton/Cook.

Mead, George Herbert. [1934] 1962. *Mind, Self, and Society.* Chicago: University of Chicago Press.

Medway, Peter, and Andrew Stibbs. 1990. "Safety and Danger: Close Encounters with Literature of a Second Kind." In *Reading and Response,* ed. Michael Hayhoe and Stephen Parker. Bristol, Penn.: Open University Press.

Newman, Denis, Peg Griffin, and Michael Cole. 1989. *The Construction Zone: Working for Cognitive Change in School.* New York: Cambridge University Press.

Polanyi, Michael. 1958. *Personal Knowledge.* Chicago: University of Chicago Press.

———. 1966. *The Tacit Dimension.* New York: Doubleday.

Pradl, Gordon. 1986. "The Experience of Myth and Myth-Making in English Education." *English Education* 18 (2): 99–106.

———. 1991. "Reading Literature in a Democracy: The Challenge of Louise Rosenblatt." In *The Experience of Reading: Louise Rosenblatt and Reader-Response Theory,* ed. John Clifford. Portsmouth, N.H.: Boynton/Cook.

Purves, Alan, with Victoria Rippere. 1968. *Elements of Writing about a Literary Work: A Study of Response to Literature.* Urbana, Ill.: National Council of Teachers of English.

Purves, Alan, and Richard Beach. 1972. *Literature and the Reader: Research in Response to Literature, Reading Interests, and the Teaching of Literature.* Urbana, Ill.: National Council of Teachers of English.

Richards, I. A. 1929. *Practical Criticism.* New York: Harcourt, Brace.

Rosenblatt, Louise. [1938] 1976. *Literature as Exploration,* 3d ed. New York: Noble and Noble.

———. 1978. *The Reader, the Text, the Poem: The Transactional Theory of the Literary Work.* Carbondale: Southern Illinois University Press.

Scholes, Robert. 1985. *Textual Power: Literary Theory and the Teaching of English.* New Haven: Yale University Press.

———. 1987. "Textuality: Power and Pleasure." *English Education* 19 (2): 69–74.

Smith, Frank. 1983. *Essays into Literacy.* Portsmouth, N.H.: Heinemann Educational.

Spencer, Margaret Meek. 1983. "Signs of Growth." In *The Development of Readers,* ed. Robert Protherough. Hull, Quebec: University of Quebec at Hull.

Squire, James R. 1964. *The Responses of Adolescents While Reading Four Short Stories.* Urbana, Ill.: National Council of Teachers of English.

Taylor, David. 1983. *Mind.* London: Century.

Tharp, Roland, and Ronald Gallimore. 1988. *Rousing Minds to Life: Teaching, Learning, and Schooling in Social Context.* New York: Cambridge University Press.

Thomson, Jack. 1987. *Understanding Teenagers' Reading: Reading Processes and the Teaching of Literature.* North Ryde, New South Wales: Methuen Australia. New York: Nichols.

Tierney, Robert, Mark Carter, and Laura Desai. 1991. *Portfolio Assessment in the Reading-Writing Classroom.* Norwood, Mass.: Christopher-Gordon.

Valencia, Sheila. 1990. "A Portfolio Approach to Classroom Reading Assessment: The Whys, Whats, and Hows." *The Reading Teacher* 43 (4): 338–40.

Vipond, Douglas, and Russell Hunt. 1989. "Literary Processing and Response as Transaction: Evidence for the Contribution of Readers, Texts, and Situations." In *Comprehension of Literary Discourse,* ed. Dietrich Meutsch and Reinhold Viehoff. New York: Walter de Gruyter.

Vipond, Douglas, Russell Hunt, James Jewett, and James Reither. 1990. "Making Sense of Reading." In *Developing Discourse Practices in Adolescence and Adulthood,* ed. Richard Beach and Susan Hynds. Norwood, N.J.: Ablex.

Vygotsky, L. S. 1962. *Thought and Language.* Cambridge: M.I.T. Press.

———. 1978. *Mind in Society: The Development of Higher Psychological Processes.* Cambridge: Harvard University Press.

Weinstein, Gerald, and Mario Fantini, eds. 1970. *Toward Humanistic Education: A Curriculum of Affect.* New York: Praeger.

Wells, Gordon. 1986. *The Meaning Makers: Children Learning Language and Using Language to Learn.* Portsmouth, N.H.: Heinemann Educational.

Wertsch, James. 1985. *Vygotsky and the Social Formation of Mind.* Cambridge: Harvard University Press.

———. 1991. *Voices of the Mind: A Sociocultural Approach to Mediated Action.* Cambridge: Harvard University Press.

Wigginton, Eliot. 1985. *Sometimes a Shining Moment: The Foxfire Experience.* New York: Doubleday.

Willinsky, John. 1991. "The Lost Reader of Democracy." In *The Experience of Reading: Louise Rosenblatt and Reader-Response Theory,* ed. John Clifford. Portsmouth, N.H.: Boynton/Cook.

Wilson, James. 1966. *Responses of College Freshmen to Three Novels*. Urbana, Ill.: National Council of Teachers of English.

Wimsatt, W. K., Jr. 1954. *The Verbal Icon: Studies in the Meaning of Poetry*. New York: Noonday Press.

Witherell, Carol, and Nel Noddings, eds. 1991. *Stories Lives Tell: Narration and Dialogue in Education*. New York: Teachers College Press.

Wolf, Denny Palmer. 1987/88. "Opening Up Assessment." *Educational Leadership* 45 (4): 24–29.

Yancey, Kathleen Blake, ed. 1992. *Portfolios in the Writing Classroom*. Urbana, Ill.: National Council of Teachers of English.

Authors

Harold A. Vine, Jr., is director of the English Education Program at New York University. He has over thirty-five years of teaching experience in working with students at the junior high school, senior high school, community college, and college levels. His major interest is in how learners—readers, writers, teachers— develop over time. He holds a Ph.D. degree in English Education from Syracuse University.

Mark A. Faust is assistant professor of English Education at the University of Georgia, where he supervises teacher candidates and conducts classes in composition and literature for young adults. An interest in understanding and empowering young adult readers continues to drive his research agenda. He is currently working with experienced teachers who are exploring nontraditional ways to assess achievement and evaluate learning based on student portfolios. His teaching and research have been greatly influenced by his eleven years of experience as a high school English teacher and his studies at New York University, where he received his M.A. and Ph.D.